WORKING WITH THE ENEMY

*This book is, quite simply, for people who have been feeling
'under attack' and want to do something about it,
once and for all.*

WORKING WITH THE ENEMY

**How to survive and thrive
with really difficult people**

MIKE LEIBLING

**KOGAN
PAGE**

London and Philadelphia

First published in Great Britain and the United States in 2009 by Kogan Page Limited

120 Pentonville Road
London N1 9JN
United Kingdom
www.koganpage.com

525 South 4th Street, #241
Philadelphia PA 19147
USA

© Mike Leibling, 2009

ISBN 978 0 7494 5467 8

British Library Cataloguing-in-Publication Data

A CIP record for this book is available from the British Library.

Library of Congress Cataloging-in-Publication Data

Leibling, Mike.
    Working with the enemy : how to survive and thrive with really difficult people / Mike Leibling.
       p. cm.
    ISBN 978-0-7494-5467-8
    1. Interpersonal conflict. 2. Conflict management. I. Title.
    BF637.I48L57 2009
    158.2--dc22
                        2009017059

Typeset by Jean Cussons Typesetting, Diss, Norfolk
Printed and bound in India by Replika Press Pvt Ltd

Contents

PART 2

Preface

All of us manage to get on with most people in most situations most of the time, and so this book is about the *really* difficult people and situations that we encounter.

Of course, every situation is different, but there are some really common patterns that emerge (or explode) time and time again. And over the years I and my clients have recognized that it's relatively simple and painless to disarm an 'enemy' using these patterns, rather than – exhaustingly – to have to deal with each situation every time it arises.

For example, it's pointless trying to deal with an 'enemy' situation while it's in the middle of exploding. We'd either fuel the flames and make it worse, or we'd get blown out of the way altogether.

And that's why it's most effective to address the *pattern* of battles, rather than each one separately, especially as they are relatively simple to identify and to deal with.

So please browse through and choose what works best for you from case studies, tips and tried and tested strategies, so that you can change these underlying patterns of behaviour once and for all.

And where the companion volume to this book (*How People Tick*, Kogan Page) details many types of difficult people and how to handle each of them, this volume will enable you to handle *yourself*.

Acknowledgements

These strategies have developed over the years and may have become hard to accredit, so I acknowledge my own major influences:

- NLP (neuro-linguistic programming);
- NVC (non-violent communication);
- TA (transactional analysis); and especially
- So-called common sense.

I would particularly like to thank:

- my clients, friends and family who continue to teach me so much;
- my publishing team at Kogan Page who truly inspire and support me, especially Jon, Martha, Andrew (who came up with the title of this book), Sarah and my patient editor Julia;
- the people who worked with me to develop The Trainset® approach ('We Can Help Absolutely Anyone To Handle Any Situation They Might Find Themselves In') especially Bill Baker, Diana Renard, Freda Gardiner, Jane Townsend, Jenny Foster, Jonathan Haigh, Jonathan Levy, Richard Cree, William Jackson, the fondly missed Mike Downes, and Robin Prior who continues to be such an inspiration;
- and the panel of contributors whose personal experiences

of difficult situations formed such a major part of the research for this book (see Research Methodology below) especially: Annie Murray, Diana Renard, Freda Gardiner, Jonathan Levy, Joyce Lucas, Kathrin Hardie, Liz Bacon, Liz Woolf, Martin McGlown, Michael Toothill, Pete Nyholm, Robin Prior, Sam Gardiner, Sarah Burns, Simon Lucas, Sophie W Gardiner, Stella M Stearston, Sue Duncan, Sara Hiom, Tor McLaren, Tricia Hartley and those others – you know who you are – who chose to remain anonymous.

Research methodology

On top of the years of developing these strategies, I additionally asked four questions of a scatter of 25 people, who all have the ability to handle many types of difficult people and situations, plus the humility to deny their ability, plus the awareness to reflect on how they could do even better.

I asked them:

1. 'What types of people have you found especially difficult/challenging/nightmarish/insertyourownwordhere to work with?'
2. 'What's worked for you, ie how exactly have you managed to handle them, or indeed handle yourself when handling them?'
3. 'When you have not handled them to your satisfaction, how come? What exactly had you done or said, or forgotten to do or say, to them or to yourself?' and
4. 'What, on reflection, might have worked even better for you?'

Their responses were varied, as you would expect, but there were some very consistent patterns that came through not only in terms of the types of people that they had found especially difficult, but also in their way of dealing with them.

Their responses are identified thus:

'Here is an example of what was said.'

'Mike'

Every word quoted is genuinely theirs and used with permission. (All names are 'Fictitious' for anonymity).

Introduction

Let's be honest, no-one knows instinctively how to 'get on' with *everyone,* so we gradually learn from each other, and we learn most usefully *not* from one-off events that have happened almost before we realize it, but from underlying patterns of behaviour. (Until the next but hopefully different pattern emerges for us to deal with, that is!)

So what do I know about Working with the Enemy? Well, professionally, I've been working as a mentor and coach for more years than I care to remember, with people and teams who have been in very different difficult situations. But I've gradually noticed some common underlying patterns that are easily identifiable and extremely fixable.

And, personally, let me sympathize as I've been there myself on many occasions. On one occasion I worked in a company where everyone was everyone's enemy. It was a toxic atmosphere where people seemed to need to put each other down in order to big themselves up.

But I've always tried to take time to reflect and understand *how* exactly situations have worked – well, or badly – and how they could be avoided or fixed in the future.

This book brings together learnings from coaching and mentoring people in 'How to get on with people we don't get on with' so that:

■ you will be able to recognize how you came to find your 'enemy' to be 'really difficult';
■ and deal with it;
■ and nip future situations in the bud, before they become 'difficult' too.

The key is not to feel overloaded with advice and ideas. If there's pressure on us to act and we don't feel comfortable, then that just makes the situation worse, doesn't it? And so this book does not tell you to Get a Goal, then Action It. It is structured as follows:

1. **The Ten Essential Survival Strategies for keeping cool, or at least cooler, in the heat of battle.** These are First Aid Techniques because the first step is not to leap into action, but to take the heat out of the situation. In this way we can approach matters with a cool, clear head.
2. **The Fifteen Toughest Types of 'Enemy'.** These are specific approaches to common situations with coping strategies for each.
3. **Getting New Information for New Ways of Moving Forward.** This is so we can now calmly collect as much information as possible about the enemy's patterns of behaviour, and our own patterns of behaviour, so that we have all the data possible for our decision making.
4. **Get Planning to Transform your 'Enemy' Situation Calmly,** ie deciding *what* we want and *how* we can get it.

Please pick and choose what suits you and, of course, only act when you feel comfortable to do so. Trust your instinct – it's got you this far and, with a clear head, it won't let you down even in the trickiest situations.

And, please, let me know (MikeLeibling@WorkingWithThe Enemy.com) how you get on.

Part 1

First things first: The Ten Essential Survival Strategies for Keeping Cool in the Heat of Battle

There are of course *many* different types of 'enemy' situations, with bosses, colleagues, staff and even outside the workplace with friends and family, but there's generally only one desire – to keep cool, keep calm and keep going.

> 'When you're going through hell, keep going!'
> *Winston Churchill*

So, presumably you're reading this because there's an 'enemy' situation you're interested in fixing, and you've not managed to fix it to your satisfaction, yet. Well, there's no need to leap into action, without thinking and planning first – after all, you've probably tried the obvious things. And there's no point in thinking and planning until you're feeling ready, which is where this part of the book comes in – getting yourself ready.

And it's a great start that you've taken responsibility for doing something about the 'enemy' situation just by picking up this book – even if a 'friend' might have thrust it into your hands in the first place!

It's really important that we don't rush off to 'fix' a situation until we feel literally 'good and ready'. And so the important first step is to apply some First Aid to start to take the heat out of the situation. In this way we can feel better – ie manage ourselves – and then prepare to manage the situation and the other person or people, with a calm mind and a cool head.

Twenty Questions

Let's start with a short questionnaire. How many of these apply to you right now?

1. Have you been feeling under pressure, under attack, or got at?
2. Have you not been sleeping well, thinking of the situation?
3. Have you felt that nothing's really helped?
4. Have you been going hot and/or cold (a lot, or a little) when thinking about the situation?
5. Have you been taking it to heart, taking it personally?
6. Has this situation been preying on your mind?
7. Have you been confused or unable to think clearly?
8. Has it been affecting other areas of your work and/or life?
9. Have you been feeling less confident?
10. Does the situation feel out of your control?
11. Do you see no light at the end of the tunnel at the moment?
12. Have you sometimes been dreading going to work or even dreading the future?
13. Has 'the enemy' been on your mind even when they're not there?
14. Have you been feeling overwhelmed?
15. Has even 'good advice' felt like a burden?

16. Have you wanted revenge?!
17. Have you wished, even a little, that they'd get fired, or worse?
18. Have you thought of leaving, if you could?
19. Has even asking yourself some of these questions been painful?
20. Are you wishing you'd acted earlier, to nip the situation in the bud?

Scores

Any one of these can feel truly dreadful, let alone all of them. So however many apply to your 'enemy' situation, rest assured that they are all very, very common and you are definitely not alone and help is at hand!

No compromises needed

The starting point in managing any situation is to manage 'me' first, before attempting to manage anything or anyone else. As long as a situation is on our mind – and we're presumably trying to keep our home life going as well – there's not much brain-space left for thinking clearly is there?

But rest assured that *nothing* in this book (or in life, in truth) requires you to take *any* steps that you're not comfortable with. Not even a little bit. And you certainly do not need to compromise your personality, your identity, or whatever else is important to you.

So here are ten essential survival strategies to start with. No doubt you will be familiar with some of them; some you may have forgotten to use; and some may be new to you, so feel free to just pick and choose.

✔ It may sound strange, but any feelings of anxiety or tension that crop up as you're doing this should be welcomed for what they are – your 'early warning' system. Don't fight them – they're definitely on your side. Take some time to question these early warning signals – not necessarily while they're signalling frantically, but in a quiet moment of reflection. Ask yourself what exactly felt wrong to you and what, therefore, could you learn from them?

1

Essential Survival Strategy 1: Communicate Extra Calmly and Clearly

It's easy to get into ways of communicating (ie thinking and speaking) that keep us from getting what we want. Here are some reminders for keeping communications calm and clear.

Survival Tip: A Great Fact is 'I Don't Know'

We know what we know. We know what we don't know. We cannot allow ourselves to be persuaded otherwise.

✔ I often find that encouraging people to say eg 'I don't know' or 'I don't know how to go about this' in a simple factual tone of voice, with a solid full stop and a silence after it, opens their eyes to a solid fact – that it feels fine to say eg 'I don't know', or 'I don't have that information', without saying internally 'and so, therefore, I must be stupid'.

✔ The factual tone of voice also makes 'I don't know' into a fact, not a fatal character flaw! It's simply about what I have or haven't got (so far) as a skill – and it's not about who I am as a human being. 'So, can you help me to get that skill, or information, please?' (And then, under my breath I might add, Because That's Your Job, Sunshine!!)

Survival Tip: Ask How, Not Why

'Why?' is a pretty useless question because in my experience the only real answer tends to be 'Because'. In most cases, what we're really searching for is to find out *how* something happened, in order to learn and then move on. It's much more illuminating to ask, for example:

■ How exactly did I get myself into this state?
■ How exactly did you reach this conclusion?
■ How precisely do you see a role for me in this project? or even
■ How exactly do you plan for us to have an enjoyable time there on holiday? (vs why (on earth?!) do you want us to go *there?*)

This form of questioning encourages people to look into their thought processes – especially when focused by words like 'exactly' or 'precisely'.

Survival Tip: Be Open and Honest

People are not mind-readers and very often when we tell them what we've been dreading telling them, they can be astonished that we hadn't told them sooner.

'More honesty and openness. Tell them what you think, what you are experiencing, eg I really want us to work well together and we need to find a formula.

'Pamela'

'When I'm tired or not feeling at my best, eg when other stuff in my personal life has taken its toll, I often simply state the obvious, eg I'm tired, so I need to take a bit of time and not rush any decision.'

'Harry'

'I feel it works best when there is no 'side', ie not trying to come across as cleverer. This – with sensitivity of course – is especially useful when managing upwards.'

'Natalie'

'I try to manage by educating: pointing out that this is an area of expertise, without specifically mentioning that it is one they don't have or listing parameters that affect decision making that I know they won't have thought of.'

'David'

'I simply invite them to get a grip on themselves and think "Why am I being this way when it's upsetting people?" '

'Victoria'

Survival Tip: Be Specific, Don't Generalize

It's so easy to *make* a generalization, isn't it? (oops!) eg 'There's no point' or 'It's hopeless.' Indeed some people generalize after just one experience, eg 'I hate that office' or 'I'll never like that person.' Similarly, some people will *take* a sweeping generalized remark, eg 'you're a bad presenter' and assume that it's true. It's not. It's an opinion based on specific experience of your performance, not of you as a person. Get some specific behavioural feedforward (*not* feedback – it's the future that matters), eg 'So how exactly would you suggest I do it next time, please?'

Ugh

I was visiting a relative in hospital, and picked up her husband on the way. We were a bit early, so I suggested stopping off for a bite of lunch. Italian? Good heavens, no! Indian? Stunned silence and look of horror. French? Absolutely not! It turned out that he'd been in the Dunkirk evacuation in World War II, and his one and only experience of 'foreign food' had been during that wartime event. And, ever since, as he said, he 'hated foreign food'.

✔ Generalizations are easy to counter by being specific, eg 'You always do...' leads to 'No, I don't always do that. Here are three recent occasions when I didn't do that. So please just tell me what you *do* want me to do, thanks.'

✔ Stick to specifics in the past tense, eg 'I've noticed that on three separate occasions you contradicted me in public and I'm asking you now to do it in private in future, please' – and make sure that you have three occasions that you can give as examples of any pattern.

Survival Tip: Don't be Negative

'For the person who always points out what will go wrong I emphasize how important their input is, and suggest that they start their input in meetings by speaking about a positive (ie something that is working) or find another way of gaining empathy. This helps to engage with the people in the room, who are then more likely to engage with the constructive input. Also I encourage them to use the word 'and' in between positives and negatives.'

'Jack'

Survival Tip: **Don't Say 'Don't' and Stop Saying 'Stop'**

Saying 'stop' or 'don't' can have the opposite effect. Try it now: 'Don't think of a pink elephant,' 'Stop worrying.' See?!

When we hear 'don't' or 'stop', our mind freezes and does whatever is said next. That's why eg 'walk slowly and smoothly' works much better than 'Don't trip and spill that drink.' We need to give a clear picture of what we *do* want.

Survival Tip: **Have your Say Calmly and Effectively**

> 'I must never allow myself to feel too small, unimportant and over-ruled to have my say!'
>
> *'Charlie'*

If we feel up to it, and prepare, we can feel able to speak to the 'enemy' directly.

> 'I've learned that asking directly is the best approach, eg "I don't feel that we've been working as productively as we might. What, in your opinion needs to happen for us to improve things? Could we maybe get together over a coffee to talk about this?"'
>
> *'Jack'*

> 'I have developed a set of questions that change their viewpoint, eg "How would you feel if you were me?"'
>
> *'Nina'*

What follows is a much simplified version of Marshall Rosenberg's non-violent communication and I've found it to be a great way to plan and rehearse what to say when wanting to confront someone with an issue without wanting it to feel either confrontational, or an issue!

Let's start with an example:

- I've noticed that I've been ignored recently compared to other people
- so I've been feeling a bit uneasy and left out
- because I want to feel part of the team, as I enjoy working collaboratively
- so I'm asking you to help me to understand exactly what your intentions are, please?

The structure behind this is quite simply:

1. having good intentions (of inviting and achieving co-operation);
2. stating calmly what I've noticed;
3. stating calmly what I've been feeling;
4. stating calmly what I need; and
5. stating calmly what I'm asking of you.

What this model has that many others don't, is a calm flow of logic based on facts, and a clear request – so avoiding the response 'So what do you expect me to do about it?'

Here's another example:

- I've heard you explain matters clearly to other team members, but snapping at me
- which can leave me feeling quite bewildered as I don't feel I deserve this
- and as I want to feel motivated and treated professionally
- can you please tell me whether you're doing this deliberately, and – if so – can we talk calmly instead about any issues you might have with my work, please?

Almost certainly this approach will open up dialogue that is focused on issues, not on personalities, and separate the *intentional* 'enemy' from the *unintentional* 'enemy'.

If the 'enemy' has acted unintentionally, then they are likely to be astonished and ashamed at the effect they've had, and want to make amends.

On the other hand if they've been acting intentionally they may well freeze a little at being found out, or fluster and bluster and not want to admit it. But in either case you will have stated your case and made a request, calmly.

You can't disagree

I worked in a shoe shop and one day I disagreed with what the kindly manager, Mr Nicholls, had said. 'You can't disagree with me, Mr Leibling,' he said, 'because if someone says something like "I think" or "feel" or "want" or "dislike," then how can anyone tell them that they don't?! But by all means tell me what *you* "think" or "feel" or "want" or "dislike" and then we can discuss it.'

Survival Tip: Make it Clear Who and What you are Trying to Benefit

Quite simply, remove any doubt by stating the obvious: for example, 'You seem to be reacting very personally but this is not for me, it's for us/the organization.'

Survival Tip: Only Challenge Gently

The most beautiful challenge I've ever experienced was a lovely smile and a gentle 'Because, Mike?'

'It's possible to challenge elegantly, by simply inviting the person to enquire deeper of themselves.'

'Harry'

Survival Tip: Put Everything in Writing

'Use e-mail as a substitute for a face-to-face relationship – difficult people remain difficult in any medium – so remove their satisfaction from seeing and hearing your reaction.'

'Harry'

'Get it all in writing (sadly).'

'Edward'

Survival Tip: Say What you Have to Say, and No More

For example, after saying 'I don't know' or 'I don't know, I'll get back to you' do not hazard a guess. You'll undermine your credibility. You'll wonder why you gave in (again!!). It's no accident that it's called 'hazarding' a guess!

Survival Tip: So you Think that Nothing will Help?

✗ If you're thinking that nothing will help, then you're caught in an exhausting dilemma, aren't you? On the one hand you really want this situation to go away. On the other hand, nothing's worked so far and it's exhausting to think of yet more good advice to follow and fail with. It's almost easier to opt out of trying new things and just stay stuck, isn't it? I don't blame you for feeling like this – in fact you're right, and it's inevitable that nothing will help you, so long as you're thinking like this.

✗ 'Nothing will help' is a self-fulfilling prophecy and unless you're a mind-reader (in which case you know exactly what'll work and you won't be reading this!) what you mean to say, I think, is 'Nothing *has* helped, and I'm exhausted by the thought of having to try, try and try again.'

✔ Take heart. This book offers you lots of ways to look anew at what *hasn't* worked for you in the past, understanding why this is so, and then enabling you to choose what *might* work for you, in your own good time. With no pressure.

✔ Be reassured that many people feel hopelessly trapped like this, as a direct result of how they speak and think – ie putting past failures into the present or future tenses, where they feel horribly solid and unchangeable, for example:

■ Nothing will work.
■ This is hopeless.
■ They'll never agree to this.
■ This person is out to get me.

✔ The accurate truth is:

■ Nothing *has* worked, yet.
■ This *has* felt hopeless.
■ They never *have agreed* to something like this, so far.
■ I've *felt* that this person *has been* out to get me.

✔ It's really easy to adjust our thinking in order to feel better, by using the past tense (and what an appropriate word 'tense' is!) for past events we didn't like, eg 'I hated it when X said such-and-such to me' rather than 'I hate it when X says such-and-such to me.' Remember, in this way we can actually choose how we think and feel, rather than have the situation choose them for us. Again. After all, it's all too easy for a careless comment or thought of ours (eg 'Nothing will work: this is hopeless') to end up as a crippling belief that we have planted and then harvested all by ourself!

✔ So please realize that it's all about realizing that in the present and in the future you're planning to think and do things differently somehow. (And that's what the rest of this book is about – some hows!)

The two villages

A traveller came down from the mountains after many years. He saw a peasant in a field and stopped to talk to him. 'I've been in the village in the mountains for a long long time, and I hated it there. The people were miserable and unfriendly. I had no choice but to leave. I thought I would try the village in the valley. What are the people like, there?' The peasant looked at him and said 'I think you'll find they're much the same.'

Later the same day, another traveller came down the mountain, and stopped to speak to the peasant. 'I've just come down from the village in the mountains and had such a great time. The people were happy and friendly and I'm sad to leave there. I thought I would go next to the village in the valley. Are the people there as nice?' The peasant looked at him and said, again, 'I think you'll find they're much the same.'

Survival Tip: Speak Their Language

'Understand their preferences and habits and work with them, not against them, eg the boss who worked only in bullet points (no point in even trying to tell a story or give lots of anecdotal back-up evidence). Join in and adapt as much as possible to their style when with them.'

'Francis'

'I must be honest about how I feel and their impact on me, but there's no point in sounding like I'm whining or too emotional, as they simply won't hear me: I need to do this by matching with their sort of language.'

'Larry'

And remember, we're only choosing our language carefully, not changing our entire personality!

Survival Tip: **Take Yourself Seriously**

'I sometimes get into a cycle of asking myself "Why should I keep bothering if they're not making any effort?"'

'Pamela'

It's useful to take questions such as 'Why should I keep bothering if they're not making any effort?' literally, and list the reasons!

2

Essential Survival Strategy 2: Keep Things Real and in Perspective

How much time and energy do I really need to spend on this? What is really important? I remember talking with a Greek gentleman about a business matter. He asked me what was the worst that could happen. I replied that we could lose the business, I could lose my job, the customer would be unhappy. 'No, Mike,' he said: 'someone could have a heart attack or a stroke or die. That's the worst that could happen. This is only business. Keep it in perspective.'

'Not "sweating the small stuff" is vital, and retaining an awareness of what is the small stuff! (I do tend to be a perfectionist, and am aware that I'm every bit as difficult to deal with as all the people I've mentioned!)'

'Patricia'

'I wish I'd won the pools the night before and told him to **** off. He might have done just that, and may well have respected me for my blunt speaking.'

'Larry'

Survival Tip: Congratulate yourself that you've Put Up with it Until Now

✗ Realize that this is not an easy situation that you've been in, so it's OK not to know how you're going to fix it yet.

✔ The past has passed. So, learn from the past. Understand the present. Choose a future. Apply the learnings. Draw a line. Move on. Don't dwell on it. Use what you can.

✔ One of the basics of NLP states that 'everyone does the best they can in the situation they're in, or think they're in, given the resources that are available to them, or that they think are available to them' so reassure yourself that no-one in the same situation would or could have done any better.

JFK

John F Kennedy had a coach, Dorothy Sarner, who helped him to stay calm by thinking something that you might like to try on for size:

'I know what I know.'

In other words, I have all the resources and information and skills and abilities that I have. But nothing more. And, importantly, nothing less either. I know what I know. Fact.

Survival Tip: Don't Assume that Everyone Should Get on Well Together

'Maybe I could stop being surprised by what shits some people are.'

'Rochelle'

Who said that everyone should get on with everyone else? If we think about true friendship, I'd say that about one in a hundred people we meet might end up as true friends. So we should assume that ninety-nine out of a hundred people might just be people we can only work with on a professional level, rather than be friends with.

And just because we work with someone doesn't mean that we have anything else in common. Some people are motivated by doing a great job. Others want to finish their work as quickly and effortlessly as possible. Some want to look good in their boss's eyes, at any cost. So we just need to focus on the work itself, or find somewhere else that's more sociable if that's what we truly need.

✔ So let's be amazed that we have so *few* enemies, statistically!

'Rapport is the tolerance of difference.'
Richard Bandler

'The art of being wise is the skill of knowing what to overlook.'
after William James

Survival Tip: **It May Not be your Fault**

✘ It astonishes me that so many organizations – even those that believe themselves to be 'caring' and charitable – are still shot through with war talk (like 'shot through,' I suppose). Personally I see no need for concepts based on aggression as I believe that we all need to be on the same side – certainly *inside* the organization (which includes departments and divisions, and even directors!). And surely we're on the same side as the clients and customers and service users that we target (oops) *outside* our organization, as we have their best interests at heart.

✘ But war talk creeps in so easily; why do we need internal 'divisions'? Why is it OK to think that clients or customers or service users can be 'targeted' when it feels so dreadful when we do it to colleagues? In this sort of environment, it's not surprising that we sometimes feel we have an 'enemy' on *our* side – trying to win by damaging or hurting others, rather than by being the best they can be.

✔ Here are some for starters, to be wary of and not take literally:

■ **Stick to your guns; at daggers drawn** – but why have these weapons in the first place?
■ **May the best person win; it's them or us** – but why? why can't we all win? That's what managers and directors are supposed to achieve, isn't it?
■ **It's a battle for survival; challenge everything** – but instead of knee-jerk reactions why not calmly and inclusively plan for success?

My co-animal

I was co-running an organization and most of my energies were spent on running my co, or so it felt. Other people tried to smooth things over, but my co seemed intent on resisting, rejecting and repelling everything that came from me. So, one day I had a heart-to-heart with them and explained, as they raised their eyes and sighed dramatically as usual, that I didn't want to work with them any more, as they seemed intent on working against me. I asked them to come up with a plan of action, and left the room. The next day I got a truly apologetic phone call from them, saying that they realized they'd been acting like an animal, as if we weren't on the same side. I accepted their apology. And, what felt even more wonderful, I then resigned! I'd just had enough and didn't want to spend any more energy starting all over again.

'Some people are just generally ignorant and you have to try really hard to cope with them but it still annoys me. It takes a lot to "train" them not to be ignorant. Normally no matter what you say or do they will just ignore you so it's not really your fault. (It would be better if parents and guardians just taught their children to be polite from an early age! It would be better for the whole world that way!'

'Edward'

Survival Tip: It's Good to Feel Bad, in a Controlled Way

✗ If we're 'feeling' eg angry or sad, or any of these other 'false feelings', we don't need additionally to 'feel' guilty or ashamed. (By the way, they're all thoughts, not true feelings. See 'Thoughts vs feelings – the great self-destructive battle-ground', page 83.)

✔ But we should 'do' our anger or sadness etc *properly*. And we should *plan* to do it properly. We should not try to suppress it any longer. So, taking 'angry' as an example, we could:

■ Plan a time and place where we can focus on what we need to do, without interruptions.

■ Determine how long would be appropriate to allow ourself to wallow properly in these thoughts and feelings, eg is this worth being *really* angry/sad for a solid five minutes? for 15 minutes? for a whole hour? for ever?

■ Determine what we are going to do *after* we've 'done' angry.

■ Keeping an eye on the time, we can then 'do' eg angry properly.

And we can, of course, plan to do it again until we've got it out of our system – after all, if we've 'been angry' (or sad or whatever) about something for years, it might take more than one session.

Survival Tip: **It's Natural to Feel Scared**

✘ It's only natural to worry about the consequences of our actions. But we can overdo it, and scare ourselves into cold panic at the thought of doing *any*thing!

✔ We should ask ourselves 'So what *exactly* am I so scared of?' – preferably while sitting upright or standing upright, and looking straight ahead to the horizon. It's easier to keep our emotions away from our analysis this way. (If you don't believe me, try looking straight ahead with a very straight back and saying 'I feel depressed' – it's not the same, is it?!)

✘ Often the answer is that we're quite naturally scared of being thought to be inadequate, incapable, or unable to stand up for ourselves, and – let's face facts – this is all true! But it's not that 'we are inadequate' full stop – it's that we *have been* inadequate at solving this ourselves, and that's why we're asking for help, please. It's not that 'we are incapable' as a human being – it's specifically that we haven't (yet) found a way of fixing this. That's all.

3

Essential Survival Strategy 3: Don't Feel Pressured into Acting too Soon

In important situations it's essential to plan your timing carefully.

Survival Tip: Go for a Gap

When a situation is erupting, that's no time for strategic discussion! When emotions are high, *our* mouth won't make much sense, and *their* ears and brain won't be receptive. And because it's exhausting to have to deal with erupting situations time and time again, it's much easier to deal with the pattern of situations, during a gap. In other words when you're being attacked by a tiger, that's not the time to start training it.

Survival Tip: Pause. Take Time.

This was the most commonly recommended strategy from our panel of contributors.

'Take time to think "Is this going to turn into one of those moments?" so I can notice a split second before it comes – so I can take deflective action.'

'Nina'

'What works best for me is to slow down to give myself thinking space and imagine what I would like to hear/see/feel if I was in their shoes. I try to have some "spacing comments" in my head, to give me time to think. These can be statements or questions: "That's interesting." "What do you think?" "Let me think about that one."'

'Francis'

'Approaching it more like a chess game, with certain moves and contingencies planned, dependent on how the encounter goes. Forward planning and being completely in possession of the necessary facts and supporting information, anticipating blockages and knowing how to overcome them.'

'Charlie'

'I should be spending more time listening and analysing what I have heard *before* giving a reply or answer. Taking time to consider what has been said or proposed and then giving a reply is much better than giving an instant response just because an instant reply is expected. Taking time to think of a reply/answer/solution is better than "shooting from the hip".'

'George'

'Taking a more planned approach and being much more analytical and less emotional in my responses.'

'Susannah'

'It's usually preferable to reach a good solution with a little more time, rather than a bad solution (eg perpetuating the battle) quickly. We should feel very confident to explain that we want to do this right, and will continue later, with an e-mail, by phone, at the next meeting etc.'

'Sheila'

'Usually I have run out of time to explain my point of view. Or I have not fully understood their thoughts/attitudes/requirements.'

'Charlie'

'I have trouble not coming across as exasperated when I am, as that doesn't help, of course. What might work better is anticipation, I suppose, ie providing the parameters etc before being asked, as that way it is less obvious that they haven't a clue and "face" is saved.'

'Harry'

And we should never underestimate how important our dignity is; oh yes, and other people's too!

'The noble art of saving face will one day save the human race.'

Hans Blix

Survival Tip: **Prepare for Tomorrow and Next Week**

When we have a lot to think about, the worst way to prepare for next week is to have Monday Morning Meetings. They allow no time to think clearly, because we are expected to leap into action immediately, and we can have spent the whole weekend worrying about what needs to be done 'next week'.

✔ The best time for Monday Morning Meetings is the middle of Friday afternoons. In that way we can have the opportunity to think clearly not only about what needs to be done, but what could be finished off *this* week instead. And we can go off for the weekend with a clear picture of the week ahead, and have a more focused weekend to enjoy.

✔ Similarly, the best time to plan the day is not when it's started already but the previous afternoon. That way, again, we have a clear picture of what's ahead of us, and we can enjoy our evening and sleep better.

✔ And, this is very obvious, but to make the most of our day, we naturally need a good night:

■ So if we've something 'on' our mind, we need to get it 'off', and we can write it down and take the paper out of the bedroom.

■ We need to do whatever's necessary to prepare for the next day – milk drinks help some people, or thinking of three nice things that happened during the day? And double checking the physical basics: a well-ventilated bedroom at a comfortable temperature? a comfortable mattress and pillow?

4

Essential Survival Strategy 4: Stop Feeling There are No Choices

Survival Tip: How to Say 'No' Nicely

I normally don't say 'No, that's impossible' as I'd rather get people to reach that conclusion for themselves. And I do that by offering three 'yeses' instead, for them to choose from. (And I'll put my preferred option in third place – see the next item!)

So eg instead of saying 'No, I can't do a full report by 3 pm' I might say 'I can let you have an un-thought-through paragraph now, or a sketchy one in one hour or a thought-through recommendation by 9 am tomorrow.' And then the important bit, 'You choose.'

And if they insist on the impossible, I'll just calmly repeat the options that *are* possible.

So, the person feels listened to and supported, as you would have helped (good employee!) if you could have helped (good for you!).

Survival Tip: Make Sure there are at Least Three Options

Sometimes we have no choice over *what* we are to do – but we always have a choice over *how* we go about it.

✗ If we feel we have *no* choice (which usually means, interestingly, *one* choice) we can feel tight in our chest and short of breath – it's called a compulsion. I *have* to do this. I have no choice. (It's a good early warning signal that we're backed into a corner with only one option and that more choices are needed.)

✗ If we have *two* choices, that's usually no better – it's called a dilemma! On the one hand this. On the other hand that. I don't know which way to turn. (Again this see-sawing is a good early warning signal that we're caught on the horns of a dilemma, and need more options to choose from.) And, incidentally, this is where mixed messages come in. We've been given two messages, and so we're in a dilemma! (The best option I've found is to give the messages back, eg 'You said X and then you said Y – can you clarify, please?')

✔ So, we generally need at least *three* options to avoid feeling trapped. And we need to have at least three *appealing* options to feel that there's some real choice.

✔ Remember that two options that we *always* have (and, yes, there are consequences for both) are:

1. to put up with the situation; and
2. to get out before things get even worse.

✔ A third option – which is clearly the most desirable in many situations – is to find a way of changing the situation for the better, somehow. The first two options may not be ideal, nor what we wanted to admit to ourself, but they are clearly strategic possibilities; aren't they?

'What might have worked is if I tried to suggest more things rather than telling them to do just very few things or only one thing because then they can experiment with their different options and find what truly works uniquely for them.'

'Patricia'

'What I do is say something like "If you don't do it then... (something bad for them)" and that usually does the trick! This is not a threat – it's offering them a calm choice, and whatever they choose, that's down to them.'

'Harry'

Survival Tip: No one has to Look Like a Loser

No-one likes to *feel* like a loser, or especially *look* like a loser in public. They'll want revenge for their humiliation, and if we think we've got an 'enemy' now, well, we ain't seen nothing yet! Let everyone save face by thinking they made their own choice.

Survival Tip: The Power of Stating the Obvious

There is a sleight of mouth pattern that is often used by hypnotists, manipulators, sales people etc, of stating two obvious things, followed by a third which is an embedded instruction that they want the subject to agree to without thinking too much.

For example, a trainer might use 'Hello, everyone – it's really cold today, isn't it? I bet you're all glad to be getting warmed up, aren't you? And really looking forward to what we'll be doing today, yes?'

Or, 'Good morning, it's nice to see you today. Thanks for coming to this car showroom – can I get you a cup of coffee or tea? While I'm doing that, feel free to have a good look around to see what appeals to you, yes?'

And the third option usually feels such a relief, doesn't it? Yes it can!

(And this structure of a sentence or question, followed by a 'tag question', eg Can't it?, Don't we? is a common way of getting someone to think they've thought something through for themselves. Until they really think it through for themselves, that is, but it may be useful for playing for time.)

So here are some examples. State the obvious. State the obvious. State what you want.

- ■ 'I'm not saying it was done deliberately, nor that anyone wanted it to turn out badly and so, as I know we all want the best, I'm going to propose X. OK?'
- ■ 'You may wonder how I can show my face after yesterday, well, it was a difficult situation for everyone, wasn't it, so how about we get on with the project and leave the emotions behind, please? So. Any ideas on what we should do next, please?'
- ■ 'I know you don't really want to do this, Mike. And you're really, really busy, I know. But – come on, Mike – I know you'll help me out, yes?' (Notice how calling someone by name makes it feel *very* compelling.)
- ■ (As a reply to the above.) 'You're right, I don't want to do this. You're right, I'm very busy. And that's exactly why I don't want to do this, because I don't have enough time to do it well. Take away projects A, B and C from me, and I can happily do it. You decide.'

And 'you decide' is a great way to hand the decision back to the person who *should* be making the decision. It's like if we have two bosses and they both demand priority, we need to explain that the priorities are theirs, not ours, and so we can't prioritize one person's priorities against another's, and since we want to do a good job for both of them, can they please get their heads together and decide, and let me have a single list?

5

Essential Survival Strategy 5: Don't Let the 'Enemy' Dwell on your Mind

Survival Tip: Avoid Uncomfortable Language

If we use language that sounds like really hard work, it will probably feel like – you've guessed it! – really hard work. For example:

- I wish I could put them back in their box.
- I could kill them.
- I need to tackle them.
- I want to stop them getting to me.
- They're getting under my skin.
- Get them off my back.
- Keep them away from me.
- Take the bull by the horns.
- Put them in their place.

It's much easier to avoid this sort of language and feel more in control.

Survival Tip: **Brush them Aside, Put them Behind you**

Some people almost shrink or collapse when under attack (usually by taking it personally) whereas others just brush it aside. Here's how they do it. When they have thoughts of how awful the situation is, how they hate this person etc, they literally wave their hand and wave aside the thoughts and the pictures in their mind's eye to put them behind them – usually with their right hand over their left shoulder – often referred to as the 'cold' shoulder, for obvious reasons. (This right–left arrangement seems to work best for about 95 per cent of us.)

And putting it behind them means putting these images and sounds into the past – because that's where they literally belong. We don't need to dwell on them any more. We need a clear mind to think about what plan of action we might develop, and 95 per cent of us use the space out to our *right* for daydreaming and planning ahead.

So, remember, Left Behind – Right Ahead. (And if it works better the other way round for you, fine!) In this way we don't get bad situations 'in our face', 'on our mind' or 'getting in our way'.

Two Buddhist priests

There were two Buddhist priests crossing a river. A woman had been swept downstream and the old priest caught her, and carried her to the bank with them. (River bank, not money bank.) They went on their separate ways and after a few days the young priest said to the old priest; 'It's no good. I can't keep quiet on this any longer. We're Buddhist priests. We're not allowed to touch women, and yet you touched that woman who was being swept downstream!' After a moment, the old priest said to the young priest, 'Yes. You're right. I did touch her. In fact, I didn't just touch her but I carried her. And I didn't just carry her, but I carried her for five whole minutes. But *you've* been carrying her for five whole days!'

Survival Tip: Stop Imagining the Worst, by Generating Choices

Instead of dreading something we imagine, based on the past, maybe we could just assume *nothing*? Or a gentle netutral 'I'm going to stay calm today, no matter what happens' instead of, for example:

> 'I'm good at setting myself up for a bad day, like coming into the car park in the morning and seeing her car and thinking "Oh no – we are set for another dreadful day."'
>
> 'Charlie'

Do *you* have a very vivid imagination when it comes to imagining the worst? Can you not see anything positive in the future for yourself because 'the worst' you're imagining is blocking your view?

If you're blessed with a vivid imagination like this, here's how to manage it:

■ Shrink your fears down into an empty picture frame in your mind's eye, making it black and white and silent as you do it, and freezing it still like a photo. Move it to the left. (Bad images should normally be kept way over to your left, or behind your left shoulder.)

■ If you think that's the worst-case scenario, imagine what could be *even* worse! And put that into a second frame, and move it to the left next to the first one.

■ In frame three put whatever you would *love* the outcome to be and – as with any pleasant pictures – move it to your right.

■ And in frame four put another favourable scenario that a favourite aunt or uncle or friend might suggest for you, and again move it to your right.

Continue filling up your picture frames until you start feeling a bit better about your options, because you're generating choices for yourself, and the 'worst-case scenario' need no longer be your only choice, ever again. Then, having put all of the unappealing pictures behind your left shoulder maybe in an imaginary album (ie give them the 'cold shoulder'), keep the appealing ones out to your right, to play with some more.

✔ Remember, at present, all you need to do is to feel better about the situation, not to fix it.

Survival Tip: Stop Thinking of Them as an 'Enemy' and They'll Stop Feeling Like One

✗ We've all heard of self-fulfilling prophesies, so the way we *think* of someone of course determines how we *feel* about them.

> '... there is nothing either good or bad, but thinking makes it so.'
> *Hamlet/Shakespeare*

✗ It might seem easier said than done but every time we think of words like 'my enemy' we conjure up imagery that reminds us of what made us feel bad in the first place, and makes us feel bad all over again.

✗ Thinking of someone as eg the 'enemy' might seem like a harmless piece of fun, to try and lighten the situation, but consider what it truly does, and how potent it is:

■ it pigeonholes a human being as 100 per cent hostile, and even if that's how it's come to feel, it's specific aspects of their *behaviour* that have struck us as negative;

■ it conjures up imagery of unpleasant situations, which in turn reignites uncomfortable feelings from the past;

■ there's a finality about the description that can make it feel as though we have to change the whole person (and how likely is that?), whereas we only need to change these aspects of their behaviour.

✔ And so we need to find another way of 'labelling' them that feels accurate but neutral (eg just their name) but maybe adding under our breath something like 'who upset me in the past but I'm going to deal with them on a professional level', which, although horribly long, can make us feel a lot better than 'the enemy' did.

✔ Or we could think of 'enemy' situations in a way that will take the sting out; for example:

- in black and white rather than colour;
- as a photo rather than a movie;
- small behind glass in a frame rather than large, loud and in-your-face.

✔ And we could label them not as 'enemy' situations but (factually) as situations that *have been* difficult and which I am going to change for the better, somehow, when ready.

✔ See. Feels a bit better already, yes?

6

Essential Survival Strategy 6: Don't Let the 'Enemy' Pull Your Strings

BULLYING

Sometimes someone really wants to 'do us down'. Maybe it's to make them feel more 'up'? Maybe they get a certain energy from bullying and harassing others? Maybe they only feel big if they make others feel small? Maybe it's a learned behaviour from their childhood, computer games or movies. It really doesn't matter where the behaviours came from; what matters is how they are handled.

As a start, I find that the actual word 'bully' is a large part of the problem as it automatically creates a 'victim' mindset by definition. And, as we all know, victims can feel so attacked, lonely, powerless and small, that they cannot possibly feel strong enough to deal with the situation.

I prefer the concepts of 'puppeteer' and 'puppet' to 'bully' and 'victim' because they describe the same scenarios but offer clearer solutions. For example, to deal with bullies one needs to address *their* behaviour, but to stop being a puppet, the solution is in our own hands! And by feeling better about what's been going on – ie simply by using a different metaphor – we can feel more able to move on.

I'm going to stick with the common terminology of 'bullying', but I encourage you to think of 'puppet' scenarios in parallel.

Survival Tip: Are they Getting at you Intentionally?

First, let's determine if the 'enemy' action has been intentional or not. Does it matter? Isn't it the end effect that we want to deal with? Yes, but if it's unintentional action, then it can often be quickly and painlessly stopped.

So what's unintentional action? It's sometimes referred to as unwitting or accidental or ignorant or unaware action. The person or people are both:

■ unaware of the effects of their action; and
■ not deliberately wanting to cause these effects.

Once the unintentional effects are pointed out to them, these people are typically horrified and ashamed of the hurt they've caused. Often they'll realize why they've been treated like an enemy, when they'd had no intention whatsoever of behaving like one.

After all, how many times when we've addressed a situation has the other person said:

■ Why didn't you tell me you felt like that?
■ I'm devastated that I'd had that effect on you. I only meant…
■ I didn't mean you to feel bad, I just… .

Survival Tip: **Check if Others are being Affected**

Some 'enemy actions may seem very personal and we may take them very personally, but are they really?

I've seen many situations where someone's been thinking for a long, long time that they've been singled out or deliberately targeted, to be bullied, belittled, picked on and pushed around, until – just about at breaking point – they've confided in someone else, only to find out to their astonishment that they're not alone: other people have been thinking and feeling the same. This can, naturally, come as a shock to the system: we have to rewrite history to accommodate the fundamental fact that it wasn't directed at us personally after all. Our conclusions about our own vulnerability, worthlessness etc were incorrect.

Question: Where does that leave us?

Answer: No longer alone. There are other puppets out there.

So are other people feeling the same or being treated the same? If we don't know, maybe we owe it to ourselves to ask around to get the information. And we can do this quite neutrally without causing problems for anyone, just by being honest and taking ownership of our own feelings, eg 'I've been feeling a bit uncomfortable with X recently. Any observations or thoughts, please?'

If an enemy's behaviour is affecting more than one person, then it's sensible to involve others in coming up with a plan to move forward. Not everyone needs, of course, to action that plan, as 'who does what' will come much later, after the 'what' has been determined.

It's now not personal as it's affected more than one person, so it's 'systemic', ie a problem in the system. How do we address this 'enemy' action, whether by an individual or a group of individuals that might have been targeting us as individuals, or as a team or group or division?

Survival Tip: Get the Organization to Sort out its own Problems

However many people are involved, there is a school of thought that says that it is not the responsibility of the individual who is being bullied or got at, to sort it out. Indeed, if one thinks of oneself as a puppet, how can we sort it out while the strings are still in place? The fact is that there is one (or more) of the organization's employees who is not being supported by the organization, and it's down to the organization to handle it. It's not the individual's responsibility to sort it out, beyond making their request for the organization to sort it out.

Survival Tip: Systemic Bullying

Some organizations deliberately encourage enmities and other so-called macho behaviours. An extreme example of this was a boss I knew who used to select one of 'his troops' for a 'sustained campaign of attrition' (these phrases are how he used to boast) to 'see what they're really made of under fire' and to make them 'bigger and stronger' when they 'got through it'. He caused, not surprisingly, countless cases of stress, illness and relationship breakdowns, without an inkling of remorse. And when, eventually, someone told him how his 'victim' was suffering, he'd ride in on his white horse and rescue the poor person and give them a raise or promotion, as if he'd never taken any 'enemy' action in the first place. Everyone knew this was going on (except the poor victims at the time) and did their best to provide support. But it was part of the so-called culture there. And, if ever people tried to change this, they were told that 'this is how we do things around here' and 'if you don't like it here, you know what to do'. And, eventually, that's what we all did. The organization no longer exists. (And, incidentally, the boss had his own series of magnificent breakdowns and then reinvented himself as a pillar of society.)

Survival Tip: Find out your Organization's Policy

At the end of the day, bullying is bullying and every organization should have an anti-bullying policy. Without one, it can become a 'he said, she said' personal battle, rather than examining and hopefully resolving the situation using predetermined 'this is what we believe and want' principles. In this way everyone is clear about what behaviours are and are not acceptable, and what courses of action are open to people if they feel bullied or are accused of bullying. If you haven't got a bullying policy, now is the time to get one before you desperately need it. Maybe speak to your HR people, or offer to form a small group to draft one. There are plenty of ideas on the internet to get you started. (And ensure that if the person who is doing the bullying is a line manager, then the policy doesn't rely on going through the line manager!)

Remember that every organization has a duty of care towards its employees and volunteers.

STOP FEELING DUMPED ON IN THE NAME OF 'DELEGATION'

Being dumped on is – frustratingly – being given a one-off task with inadequate time and instruction for doing it well. It is, importantly, very different to delegating, as we feel dumped on, not entrusted and/or coached. But as someone dumps something on us, and disappears into the distance claiming 'I'm delegating this to you' we need to do two things. First, we need to do it as best as we can – now is not the time to argue. And second, we need to meet with the person who did this to us – after the panic is over – and calmly find a different way of working.

This might help. True delegation involves training or coaching someone to manage a category of tasks, rather than one-off panics, and to take responsibility for the category, with support as needed. It's very similar to 'deputizing'. Have a look at this approach to delegation, maybe show the 'dumper' and then discuss with them how you can learn to take this category off them, to ease their load. But, essentially, see what's been missing for you, to focus discussion.

Survival Tip: Get them to Delegate, Not Dump

1. Get a full explanation of exactly *what* is needed, in what form, for what purposes, and within what deadlines. But you don't need to be told *how* to do it, unless that is critical from a process or health and safety perspective. (How you yourself do something may not be the same as for people with different abilities, skills and experience.)

2. Consider what exactly the brief is, and play it back to, and agree it with, the delegator.
   NB It is absolutely essential to agree the *what*, before starting on the *how*.

3. Now consider, and then discuss:
   – *how* you plan to achieve this;
   – what resources/training you'll need;
   – what support/supervision you want;
   – what authority you'll need;
   – and who needs to be informed that you have this authority.

4. Agree on the reassurance you both want that the project is going to be on track, eg 'I'd like to check in with you every five minutes, please?' 'Well that would drive me mad. How about every half day to begin with?'

5. And on completion discuss:
   - learnings for each of you;
   - feedforward/next steps.

7

Essential Survival Strategy 7: Don't Automatically Believe Other People

We need to remember that 'advice' is other people's opinions, offered because of what we did do, didn't do, said or didn't say, and flavoured by their own agendas. They are not universal truths, and they're easy to challenge gently, eg 'So you didn't like my presentation. I'm sorry. So how exactly would you like me to do it next time, please?'

So if they've had a pattern of being destructively critical, I'd go to them well in advance of the next event and tell them eg 'You've had a lot of problems with my presentations recently. Please tell me what exactly you're expecting from me this time?'

And if – as can often happen – they can't answer and brush me aside with eg 'Surely you know what I want?' I'd take them literally, eg 'I had thought so, but I want to be sure, so would you please spell it out for me?'

And if – as can again happen – they brush this aside with eg 'I really don't have time for this right now' then I'd brush it right back with eg 'OK, but to avoid another "situation", when *will* you have time, to spell out clearly once and for all exactly what you're expecting, please?' And then I'd add eg 'I think it'll take about 10 minutes. I can come to you. When exactly would suit you?'

And, if necessary, I'd confirm all this in an e-mail. It's my responsibility to get what I need.

Incidentally, I find it helpful *not* to think of The Truth but of there being several types, for example:

◼ the 'truth' we see, hear, feel, taste and smell through our five senses;
◼ the 'truth' we feel deep down instinctively (our sixth sense, maybe);
◼ the 'truth' we are told; and
◼ the 'truth' we discover and reason for ourself.

I'm a big fan of the last one above, in case you hadn't guessed, because what is true for me and my situation is not necessarily true for other people in other situations. I'm willing to do my research and listen to advice, but at the end of the day I need to be true to myself.

And so I've become sceptical and questioning about pretty much all that I hear and see, and want to work it out for myself. For example, in my experience, we should trust no more than half of what we see, and a tenth of what we hear. Of course we can gratefully thank people who offer advice to us, but we're thanking them only for their offer. We don't need to do as they say, as opposed to what we feel.

BEWARE GOOD ADVICE

We have all taken on board Good Advice from parents, teachers and other (hopefully) well-meaning role models – but perhaps we weren't aware that advice generally applies, or applied, only to a very specific situation, based solely on the advisor's own experiences, at a specific point in time, and may not be The Truth it appears to be.

Survival Tip: **Getting and Using Advice**

✗ Only 'accept' other people's advice (other than for obvious safety and health purposes, of course) as opinions, data or information from another perspective.

✔ Ask for specific examples to help you to understand clearly where they're coming from.

✗ Don't enter into any discussion with them about how you might or might not use their advice.

✔ Just thank them genuinely, then change the subject to avoid discussion. If they're insistent to know what you're going to do, then explain that you're going to do a lot of thinking first on all the good advice you've been given. Thank you. Full stop.

✗ Beware – some good advice (eg 'You should…') can pop up later as powerful beliefs (eg 'I should…'), which can feel like powerful compulsions.

✔ So whenever you find yourself saying or thinking 'I should…' or 'must' or similar, notice that (unless it's a 'Sensible Should', eg 'I should leave now to get to Birmingham on time') it's often followed by its own 'but…', which makes it very hard to move forward.

> 'If I do what I "should", then I feel I'm not being true to myself, but if I don't, then I feel I'm letting other people down. Should I do what they say, or what I feel?'
>
> 'Francis'

✗ So don't let a Should overpower your very important 'but…' instinct.

✔ Question the Should by asking yourself 'Who says?' or 'What exactly would happen if I didn't?' (Obviously if it's an 'I shouldn't' rather than an 'I should' you can use 'So what exactly would happen if I *did*?' And of course you can adjust all of these for 'I mustn't' or 'It's not right for me to...' or other variations on the theme.)

✗ Protect yourself from future 'shoulds', 'musts' etc by hearing them as 'maybe I could consider...' or 'perhaps, in their opinion, I might...', which will help you to smile even more genuinely as you thank them for their suggestion (and leave it at that and *don't* discuss it!)

✔ So-called Good Advice comes from many different directions, different lives and different times, so I personally always want to have at least three pieces that I'd be happy with before I begin to choose.

✔ Advice (and this is just my opinion, you understand!) is best given as 'maybes' and 'perhapses' – ie simple bits of information with the lightest possible touch, and trailing away at the end of the sentence... to allow the person to take it on board, or not, as they choose. In that way it will get taken on board as their own idea (because that's what it will have become) and not as yet another 'should' or cushion... .

Beware cushions

I was at a conference run by the Samaritans and there was a great role play of how to be a Samaritan, and how not to be.

The first part – the How Not To – showed a distressed woman carrying many cushions and a big black cloud. 'I feel so low,' she said, at which point the so-called Samaritan interrupted her: 'Oh, well, you should go to the doctor' – and he pushed another cushion onto her, with 'Good Advice' written on it. 'But I'm a single parent and childcare is so expensive,' she added. 'Never mind, we'll give you the address of Social Services,' interjected our so-called friend, pushing another 'Good Advice' cushion onto her. So by the end of this encounter she stumbled away with even more cushions, and her big black cloud.

The second part – showing how it *should* go – started with the Samaritan listening to her reasons for feeling so low and, as she was talking, she slowly handed him one of her cushions with 'Feeling Isolated' on it.

After a long silence, he asked her whether she ever felt suicidal. There was a long pause, both on the stage and in the audience, as she eventually whispered, 'Yes' and she slowly handed him a tiny black cushion with the word 'Death' written on it.

And by the end of this role play she walked away with a few fewer cushions as she handed the Samaritan her big black cloud, to reveal a slightly smaller, slightly less-black cloud that she took with her, saying 'Thank you. I feel a little lighter now... .'

The audience was rapt, waiting to see how on earth they would conclude this, when the Samaritan-in-charge walked briskly onto the stage, took the big black cloud and the excess cushions from our Samaritan, and patted him on the back, leaving him ready for his next caller.

QUESTION EVERYTHING

Most 'enemy' situations have less to do with who we are as a person, than not having had decent data to work with in the first place. If we had had useful information on the situation, we'd have understood how to fix it by now. We should find out the facts for ourselves before drawing conclusions or going along with other people's conclusions. We can ask ourselves 'what else might be the reason for them saying that?' or 'Why might they be saying that, really?'

No more thanks, 'friend'

I remember being told by a 'friendly' colleague that another colleague, 'Jim', was trying to undermine me and I should stay away from him wherever possible. I gradually noticed, which I hadn't before, that Jim was indeed giving me funny looks, keeping me out of meetings and generally giving me the cold shoulder. Eventually I went to Jim and asked him what was going on. He told me that our so-called 'friendly' colleague had said on several occasions that I had problems that were affecting my work and that he should give *me* a wide berth. I explained to Jim that the only problem I had was with my 'friendly' colleague, it seemed, who we decided was manoeuvring for promotion, at my expense!

I now always go to the horse's mouth to understand first-hand what the situation is. (And, since you ask, I subsequently went to my 'friendly' colleague when he was with a few other people and told him that Jim and I had had a long talk and that he needn't worry himself with my performance issues or problems any more, thank you.)

Survival Tip: Beware Little Red Riding Hood (ie Beware 'Good Advice' Masquerading as 'Truth')

I've long been fascinated by the apparently simple fairy tale of 'Little Red Riding Hood', and how – when we deconstruct it – it's such a dangerous model of believing what we're told!

Little Red Riding Hood

Once upon a time there was a little girl called Little Red Riding Hood who lived in the woods with her mother. One day, her mother told her that her grandmother was ill, and she was to take a basket of food to her, but she was to be careful and steer clear of wolves. On her way, she was spotted by a wolf and earmarked by him as his lunch, or to be precise, dessert. He somehow knew that she was going to her grandmother, got there first, devoured grandmother as his main course, and then dressed up in her clothes to await Little Red Riding Hood. To cut a long story short, the wolf had her as his dessert, and a wood-cutter who had been following our heroine killed the wolf and cut open his belly to release the grandmother and the little girl, who then promptly went outside, got a large stone and put it in the belly of the wolf.

Now, let's be just a little sceptical of *everything* here. If we think for ourselves about what we've been told – and in organizations this doesn't always happen! – we'll ask:

- How on earth did the wolf know where Little Red Riding Hood was going?
- How was he able to swallow, whole and unharmed, both an old lady and a child? How big were he and his mouth? Seriously?!
- How could he have the physical dexterity to dress himself in grandma's clothes?
- Let alone with grandmother undigested inside him?
- How could he understand what Little Red Riding Hood was saying, and speak her language, and imitate her grandmother's voice?
- How could a mother send her daughter into the woods where she knew it was dangerous, with wolves? What does this say about her parenting skills?
- How could the mother not go with the child, or indeed on her own, to see her own mother? What does this suggest about her relationship with her own mother?
- What little girl would leave the scene of such a trauma and return to it, let alone with a large stone, let alone putting it into the open belly of a wolf? (This is a very unusual child, not the innocent we might have assumed, no?)

■ How – honestly – could a little girl not know the difference between her own grandmother and (you've got there before me!) a wolf?

And that's just based on the short version of the story!

Believe nothing until it feels right to you. That's my 'advice'.

Survival Tip: **Beware So-Called Wisdom**

There are many common sayings that we might have swallowed in the past and might just want to think twice about in future. Our own life is for real, not a fairytale, and we have to use our instinct, ask questions and know that no one will look after our own interests as well as we can – ie not by uncritically accepting everything we see or hear.

Which of these have you, maybe, been accepting without question?

■ **A bad workman blames his tools** – but these tools might have been foisted onto us by someone else, who then denies all responsibility.
■ **A bird in the hand is worth two in the bush** – but if you need the two in the bush, what use is the one in your hand?
■ **A change is as good as a rest** – so the more overloaded we become, the more rested we are?!
■ **A leopard cannot change its spots** – but it can change its direction and its mind.
■ **All's fair in love and war** – not if people get hurt, it's not.
■ **All's well that ends well** – even if people are hurt in the process?
■ **Better late than never** – but some things will never succeed, and should be nipped in the bud.

■ **Better the devil you know than the devil you don't know** – but better still, no devils, thank you.

■ **Discretion is the better part of valour** – but speaking up for oneself, discreetly if need be, avoids the need for valour or drama later.

■ **Do unto others what you would have done unto yourself** – but they may not need or like what we like, so ask them and then Do unto others what *they* would have done unto *them*!

■ **Don't count your chickens before they're hatched** – ie never estimate what a likely outcome might be? Really?!

■ **Don't judge a book by its cover** – Don't judge a book *only* by its cover?

■ **Don't rock the boat** – that's ridiculous – it's an 'enemy' situation – it *is* rocked and I need to take control of it myself, to *un*rock it.

■ **Every person is the architect of their own fortune** – but builders can really make a mess of it if they're not supervised closely.

■ **Facts speak louder than words** – but who speaks the so-called facts, and what's their agenda?

■ **Familiarity breeds contempt** – and expertise, elegance, shared understandings, wisdom, calmness.

■ **Give someone an inch and they will take a mile** – only if we're not clear about why we're giving it, and what they're to do with it.

■ **Give someone enough rope and they will hang themselves** – or hang me!

■ **Great minds think alike** – Einstein and Churchill? Really? What about the context and the need?

■ **Great oaks grow from little acorns** – not if they're left on a shelf or not fed or watered, as we as people need nurturing too.

■ **Half a loaf is better than none** – but maybe it's better to wait for the bricks to arrive if we're going to build a wall.

■ **Honesty is the best policy** – but it doesn't need to be brutal honesty.

■ **If at first you don't succeed, try, try and try again** – but why not consider trying something different?

■ **Ignorance is bliss** – so, ignoring a situation makes it blissfully improve or go away?

■ **In for a penny, in for a pound** – absolute nonsense – this is how gamblers ruin themselves and others – I'm happy with my penny, thank you.

■ **It is always darkest before the dawn** – but how do we know it's at its darkest when we're right in it, and it's still getting darker and darker and darker? The solution is early illumination.

■ **It takes all sorts to make a world** – but we don't have to take everything these sorts throw at us.

■ **It's no use crying over spilt milk** – but we can say 'Sorry' or 'I think it would be fair for you to clean it up rather than expect me to.'

■ **Knowledge is power** – and knowing that we need to handle a person or situation gives *us* the power to devise and execute a plan.

■ **Learn to walk before you run** – or, for some people, learn to run a team or an organization before you run it or us into the ground, please.

■ **Let bygones be bygones** – but if we're still seething about something, that's because we've not taken the learnings from the situation and achieved closure with the other people and within ourself.

■ **Lightning never strikes in the same place twice** – but enemies do, once they've spotted the weakness.

■ **Look before you leap** – for goodness sake could they please just walk and talk and listen occasionally, instead of leaping all the time, and expecting others to do the same.

■ **Many hands make light work** – unless the task demands single-handed concentration, without interference.

■ **Never put off till tomorrow what can be done today** – unless an extra day's planning and thinking will help us to do it better, or, if we enjoy doing it today, we can do it again tomorrow!

■ **Never say die** – but some people ignore the obvious, that the project is all but dead, and further effort is pointless.

■ **No news is good news** – except when the silence is filled with suspicion, gossip and rumour.

■ **Nobody is perfect** – but if someone makes the same mistakes over and over again, this excuse is inappropriate.

■ **Opportunity seldom knocks twice** – unless we keep in touch with the person who knocked.

■ **Out of sight, out of mind** – not if someone or something's preying on our mind all the time.

■ **People who live in glass houses should not throw stones** – but if we like going to the lake and find that gentle ripples are soothing, then why not?

■ **Practice makes perfect** – but people have different natural aptitudes and preferences and intelligences so, to be personal, however much I do piano practice, I doubt that this can always be true.

■ **Pride comes before a fall** – or before a job well done.

■ **Revenge is sweet** – so why is it also described as bitter?

■ **Spare the rod and spoil the child** – but we're all colleagues now – even bosses – and we will not accept being treated as children, let alone being physically or mentally abused.

■ **Sticks and stones will break my bones but names will never hurt me** – oh yeah?! Some of us may just laugh off name-calling, whereas others find it a hugely abusive form of mental bullying at a very personal level.

■ **The end justifies the means** – but the end is never truly the end, and surely they'll want us to feel motivated on the next project, and the next one, no?

■ **The pen is mightier than the sword** – poison pen letters?

■ **The proof of the pudding is in the eating** – or – before it's too late – in the recipe, in the preparation, in the oven?

■ **The road to hell is paved with good intentions** – in reality the road to *everywhere* can be paved with intentions, good or bad, so we'd be well advised to check out the directions in advance, and on more than one map, and consult others who've made that journey.

■ **There is no fool like an old fool** – so let's stop fooling ourselves and condoning our own foolish behaviour (ie not addressing situations that we know need addressing).

■ **There is safety in numbers** – but don't crowds get massacred too?

■ **Time is money** – and rushing around blindly can waste a lot of both.

■ **To err is human, to forgive divine** – come on, to forgive is very human too.

■ **Too many cooks spoil the broth** – unless you need it to be well prepared, and on time.

■ **Variety is the spice of life** – but variety for variety's sake can wreak havoc in an organization.

■ **Virtue is its own reward** – except if we'd prefer praise or recognition or promotion or a pay rise perhaps?

■ **When in Rome, do as the Romans do** – yes we should fit in to different situations, but we should always still be ourselves.

■ **When the cat's away, the mice play** – and who says we're not supposed to enjoy what we do, rather than live in fear?

■ **Where there's a will, there's a way** – but not if your will gets in my way, for your own selfish reasons, thank you!

■ **You scratch my back and I'll scratch yours** – but maybe you are planning to stab me in the back rather than just scratch it?

8

Essential Survival Strategy 8: Don't Let the Past Block your Future

Survival Tip: Address Issues Before they Grow Big and Scary

It's useful to assume that an 'enemy' event is the start of, or part of, a *pattern* as it's easier to deal with a pattern, in a calm pause, rather than having to deal with a series of events when they're actually happening.

> 'Taking action earlier – particularly in cases where people were unreliable or tended to blame others – is more effective than assuming that it's an isolated incident.'
>
> *'Larry'*

> 'It's a false economy to save time "now" by accepting the challenging behaviour because one can potentially end up having to "suffer" the behaviour for years. And it's harder to change behaviour further down the line – so it's far better to attend to the repairs as the train has just left the station.'
>
> *'Patricia'*

'The area for improvement for me is to recognize early that a situation needs to be handled in a more conscious or aware way.'

'George'

✔ Some situations do sometimes actually resolve themselves or go away on their own. Maybe the 'enemy' leaves. Perhaps there's a new boss who fires the 'enemy' and apologizes profusely on behalf of the organization. (Hah! As if!) There's nothing wrong with hoping that the whole situation will 'go away', of course, but we need to take responsibility for doing *something*, otherwise we'll continue being the person that's being done to, not the person who's doing the doing.

✔ A stitch in time *does* save nine, preventing battles becoming full-blown wars. And, as they say, even though the best time to plant a tree is twenty years ago, the next best time is now.

✔ And even though there's no rush to plan exactly what we'll do or how we'll do it, we do need to know that unless we take our future into our own hands, it's not our future.

'I didn't handle her at all well for years until I'd had enough of being pushed around, and so I shouted that at her! It really shook her much more than I'd expected and she backed off. We had an uneasy truce for the rest of the time we worked together. Of course it would have been much better to voice my disagreements reasonably and much earlier but that didn't seem like a viable course of action at the time – confidence in tatters. Another problem with her was that she was one of those people who can talk endlessly and you have no idea at the end of it what they've said! It was just meaningless managerial jargon. I used to have to ask her what exactly she wanted me to do, after she'd spent half an hour – as she thought – telling me. It used to infuriate her, and so she didn't encourage further openness. Failing that, in retrospect, shouting at her much sooner would have been more comfortable in the long run.'

'Larry'

Survival Tip: **It'll be All Right**

However professional we might be at work, we're all human and a simple human reassurance can help enormously, even from outside the workplace, eg I have a friend who has calmed me many times in the past by saying, 'It'll be all right, Mike, it really will be,' even though he doesn't know what's wrong, and even though I don't know *how* it'll be all right – I feel that it really will be! And I just have to imagine him saying it, for me to feel calmer.

> 'It gives you the power to find the solution yourself, just by virtue of someone saying it'll be all right.'
>
> *'Edward'*

> 'Whenever I've resigned from previous jobs I've felt such a sense of relief – it's a fantastic feeling of freedom second only to winning the lottery, I imagine! So whenever times are tough I imagine that I have resigned and feel relief that it'll soon all be over. Because it will be.'
>
> *'Patricia'*

Survival Tip: **Keep Past Events in the Past**

If not, you will not only perpetuate the bad feelings but also create a poor self-image. For example, try avoiding phrases such as 'I am stupid' or 'This'll never work for me' in favour of 'I did something stupid' or 'This has never worked for me.' Feel the difference? Here are some more examples: how do the first and second statements in each pair feel to you?

A. They always seem to be getting at me.
B. They always seemed to be getting at me.

A. They make me feel so small.
B. They always used to make me feel so small.

A. This will never work for me.
B. This has never worked for me.

The B examples have less emotion attached, as they are about our behaviours, rather than about us as a continuing victim.

So, simply by putting past events in the past tense, we can feel better – ie continue discussions about who said or did what to whom and where and when – rather than hold our breath by 'taking it' personally.

9

Essential Survival Strategy 9: Don't Take it Personally – Take it *'Behaviourally'* Instead

When I was a child, and long afterwards to be honest, kindly people used to say to me 'Don't take it so personally, Mike!' or 'Don't take it to heart.' I knew that what they were saying was well meant, but I felt like screaming back at them 'Great advice, thanks, but *how*?!' Well, here are some strategies and I particularly commend the longest one below – neurological levels. Of course, people may well think, for example, we're 'stupid' or 'lazy' or 'beneath them' but that's just their opinion, in shorthand, not a fact. And that opinion is only based on what we did or didn't do, not on who we are as human beings. So instead of shrivelling inside we can ask useful forward-looking questions of ourself, or indeed of them, such as 'What did I do or say, and what would be preferable next time, please?'

'What you think of me is not who I am.'

The Trainset® Group

It's vital that everyone knows how not to take things personally because we can literally feel diminished at the very deepest level and since we are all equals, none of us deserves to be regarded as superior or, therefore, inferior. (Sure, different people get paid more or less, depending on how the organization values their so-called skills, but that is no measure of their value as a human being.)

I now never take things personally, even praise – for what use is it for someone to tell us eg we're wonderful, without telling us what, in their opinion, we were wonderful *at*?! It's much more useful to take things behaviourally, ie what was said or done or not said or not done.

Because if they liked what we did, we could do it again. And if they didn't like it, then of course we can do or say things differently next time, without losing face.

Survival Tip: Keep Focused on the Task Professionally, Not Emotionally

I find that sitting or standing with a straight back helps, not slumping into a victim-posture. And looking the person in the eye (or at the tip of their nose will look the same to them) helps me to be direct and clear.

> 'I allowed them to get under my skin, usually by taking things too personally and not detaching feelings and the need to be liked from the situation. I allowed myself to feel disempowered, weak, even scared of the consequences of "going against" or challenging someone. It is probably when I've not been sure enough of myself, my position, or had the courage of my convictions that's been the major reason for not handling them successfully.'
>
> *'Edward'*

> 'When I've not handled them well it's been by becoming resentful and bitchy, losing perspective on the situation and seeing every little word or gesture as a put-down... ("He raised his eyebrow in a threatening manner...").'
>
> *'Jack'*

'What hasn't worked is when someone – accidentally or deliberately – treads into a sensitive area of mine and I bite back before I think clearly. It happens sometimes if I am feeling tired or stressed.'

'Nina'

Survival Tip: Take Things Behaviourally Instead of Personally: the Neurological Levels

The most simple and powerful way I know not to take things personally, is to use the approach known as the neurological levels, which maps how we *do* take things personally and how we can do things differently, therefore. It was developed by Robert Dilts from work by Gregory Bateson, and as with any model like this, there are debates about how it should be presented and used, but this simplified version has, I've found, worked perfectly well.

Bear with me, as we explore this. Imagine one sentence but with a different word emphasized each time, and as you try this, notice the different thoughts and feelings each one brings up for you:

I can't do that *HERE.*
I can't do *THAT* here.
I can't *DO* that here.
I *CAN'T* do that here.
I can't do that here.

Level 1 – I can't do that *HERE*

Most people find no particular feeling here, ie 'It's no big deal, I could do that somewhere else, or some other time, or with different people.' This level is called the **Environment**. It's where and when we do what we do.

Level 2 – I can't do *THAT* here

This similarly, carries no particular feelings with it, ie 'I might be able to do something else here, but I can't do that!' This level is called **Behaviours**. It's what we do.

Level 3 – I can't *DO* that here

This next level gets more interesting. For most people 'I can't *do* that here' just feels neutral, eg 'I'm sorry you want me to speak in Japanese, but I can't do that. I don't have that particular skill.' This is about our **Abilities**, our **Skills** and **Knowledge**. We've either got it or we haven't. Fact. Some people, however, stray into the next two levels, by adding something like 'but I should be able to, I suppose…?' and all sorts of emotions get stirred up as they, you've guessed it, take it personally. This is *how* we do what we do.

Level 4 – I *CAN'T* do that here

This is the level of our **Values** and **Beliefs** and there's a power behind it, a need to push away the world, or at least the person whose suggestion has violated some deeply held value or belief of ours. And this is a very typical level at which enmity occurs – where there is a clash of values and beliefs. This is *why* we do what we do.

Level 5 – *I* can't do that here

And then, last but never least, there's our **Identity** – '*I* can't do that here.' Someone else might be able to, but *I* can't. Please don't even put me in that position – and we often put a hand to our chest as we try to push ourself (= our self) back from this very personal situation. This is who we are, as we do what we do.

So, in a nutshell, we have five levels that feel different in our neurology:

1. **ENVIRONMENT** – *where* we do what we do (I can't do that *here*);
2. **BEHAVIOURS** – *what* we do, in that environment (I can't do *that* here);
3. **ABILITIES, SKILLS, KNOWLEDGE** – *how* we do what we do (I can't *do* that here);
4. **VALUES, BELIEFS** – *why* we do what we do (I *can't* do that here);
5. **IDENTITY** – *who* I am as I do what I do (*I* can't do that here).

The first three typically carry no feelings with them as we're not at risk. The fourth carries the feeling that our values and beliefs are being attacked. And the fifth feels as if our very identity is exposed to attack. What great early warning signals these last two are, alerting us to how we are interpreting events (ie personally!). And we can 'take it' personally *even if that's not intended*, for example if we have a disagreement over facts, or if someone tries to bully us and 'make' us feel small.

> 'Criticism can make me defensive – so what I do is to focus on outcomes in an unemotional way.'
>
> *'Keith'*

> 'Separate the behaviour from the message, with an emphasis on the content in an objective way.'
>
> *'Susannah'*

So, how do we *not* take things personally? As you've probably worked out, it's by avoiding the levels of our Identity (5) or even more powerfully, someone else's opinion (4) or our own opinion (4) of our identity (5). All we need to do is to move to one of the first three levels. For example:

■ And so what exactly you're asking me to do is...? (level 2)
■ So when exactly can you explain the rest of this to me? (1)

■ So it's not that you think (4) I am a bad presenter (5) but that I need to get some presentation skills training? (3)

I love you and hate what you did

When I was leaving a restaurant I passed a couple consumed in a massive hug and kiss. And as they were embracing, the man said to the woman 'If you ever say anything like that about me again, in front of other people, I'll get really upset. OK darling?' And he gave her a genuinely warm kiss, took her arm affectionately, and the two of them walked back to their table. A clear example of 'I love you (level 5) very much but I hate (4) what you just did (1 and 2).' And then – literally, in this case – moving on. This is a good example of a deliberately mixed message.

ESSENTIAL SURVIVAL STRATEGIES FOR EACH NEUROLOGICAL LEVEL

1. Environment – *Where* we do What we do – I Can't do that *Here*

■ Deliberately choosing the most potent time and place to speak to someone can have the most impact on the message, and the wider message, eg saying 'I'd really like us to sit down and settle our differences' will have a very different effect when said in a public place with other people knowing we've made this approach, compared to saying it in private with no one else around.

■ We should ensure that we are as physically comfortable as possible, as making an adjustment at any one neurological level will affect all of the others as well, eg we could literally stand up to them, if they are hovering over us while we're sitting at our desk; or we could say that we'll come and see them in their office once we've finished what we're concentrating on and can focus on what they need.

■ And, if we choose to have our say publicly, it's sometimes a good idea if we subsequently go and offer an olive branch in private, eg choosing to address an 'enemy' with others around ensures that the situation is brought into the open more than a 'quiet' word could do, and the quiet word can indicate a willingness to continue working professionally together.

2. Behaviours – *What* we do, in that Environment – I Can't do *that* Here

■ Do something different to take some control, eg approach them to ask something when it suits you, instead of waiting for them to approach you when it suits them.
■ Surprise the 'enemy' by not doing something they were expecting, eg instead of automatically saying 'yes, certainly' maybe stay silent and then offer to get back to them with a plan of how it can best be achieved.

3. Abilities, Skills, Knowledge – *How* we do what we do – I Can't *do* that Here

■ This is about your skills, not who you are. If criticized for an aspect of your work, take them at their word and admit you're clearly needing some skilling up (none of us was born with all the skills and knowledge we'd later need, were we?) and ask them which courses they'd recommend, or whether they'd be willing to coach you or mentor you (and for a double whammy you could ask them this in public where you'd be seen to be taking control, nicely).
■ Be confident about the skills you haven't got – yet – and about saying you don't know how to do something. It's a great self-awareness to be able to do this, and to role model this confidence to others.

4. Values, Beliefs – *Why* we do What we do – I *Can't* do that Here

■ State the obvious about what's important to you (because it's obviously not obvious to them) as the strength of feeling at this level is a powerful communicator in itself, eg 'It's really important to me to do a job well, and not hand it over rushed or incomplete, so I'm really keen to think through how I can best fit this in, thanks. I'll get back to you in 15 minutes.' and our strength of feeling is made clear by the unarguable assertion of what's important (ie doing a job well, in this case).

■ It's a fundamental part of most models of mediation and dispute resolution to find some shared values, eg 'Even though we're divorcing, we both want the best for the children, don't we, so how can we achieve that for them?' or 'I really need to feel that I do my job properly, and I'm sure that you do too, yes? So why don't I think this through so that we can discuss it in about 15 minutes.' And then moving to levels 1 and 2... 'Will you come back here, or shall I bring it to you?'

■ And – no matter what we say or do at this level, it'll be obvious to everyone that we value working together with other people without enmity.

5. Identity – *Who* I am as I do what I do – *I Can't* do that Here

■ We don't have to 'take it' personally. We can use our internal translator here, eg when someone says 'You are stupid' we can hear it more accurately as 'I don't like something you did or said.' So we can answer calmly at level 2, eg 'Whatever it was I did or said that made you take this so personally, please rest assured that I did not intend for you to be so very upset. So what exactly would you prefer me to do next time? Just tell me, please?' (And again it has a whole new level of impact, literally, when this is done in public.)

■ Tell them you're not taking it personally. Calm and measured straight-talking can work much more powerfully in public and so should be used with care, but it might be very useful here if other people have been feeling similarly under attack, eg 'I want you to know that when you call me or other people "stupid" it's really hard for me to understand what's upset you so much, that you launch into a personal attack. Am I so unapproachable that you can't have a straight person-to-person discussion of what exactly you need from me?'

'I don't even take compliments personally. It may be very nice to hear "You are wonderful" opinions [level 4] about me [level 5], but in the workplace they're no use at all until we understand what exactly we've said or done [level 2] that has pleased them. So I normally thank them for their compliment and then enquire "And what exactly were you pleased about, please, because unless I know, I might not be able to do it again!"'

'Melissa'

'I am enough'

Some people feel 'under pressure' or 'stressed out' as they 'strive to be perfect'. This story touches me deeply.

Carl Rogers, the psychotherapist, was asked how come he was so successful at what he did. He replied 'Before a session with a client I remind myself that I Am Enough. I am not "perfect" and in any case, "perfect" is not human, and would not be enough. But I am human, and there is nothing that this client can say or do or feel that I cannot feel in myself. So I can be with them. I am enough.'

10

Essential Survival Strategy 10: Look After Yourself

Good *thinking* is impossible when bad *feelings* flood our attention. And if the bad feelings are really crippling then a visit to the doctor may well be advisable. (We don't have to take their advice, after all!) But there are many other things that we can do that will help.

Survival Tip: **Avoid 'To Do' Lists**

Lengthy 'to do' lists can make the road ahead seem even more daunting, and they generally don't work because they ignore at least nine other necessary categories for causing change:

1. things to do;
2. things to say;
3. things to stop doing;
4. things to stop saying;
5. things to think;
6. things to stop thinking;
7. things to believe;

8. things to stop believing;
9. things you need;
10. things you no longer need.

And it's often true that more progress is achieved by what we *stop* doing than by what we actually do:

'I went to the doctor the other day. I told him that whenever I put my arms up like this, it hurt. So he told me to stop doing it!!'

Tommy Cooper, comedian

Survival Tip: Call Them Whatever Feels Better to You (Inside)

'These people tended to ignore me. Just didn't want to co-operate. So I managed without them even though life would have been easier if I was able to work with them. I was always very polite when I saw them. Said all the "right things", eg "Oh, I do like your dress," "I hope you had a good holiday." Strange not to be acknowledged. One cow, whenever I walked past her in the corridor, completely ignored me, even if I smiled and looked at her. She always wore black. I called her "the black witch". Made me feel better.'

'Natalie'

'Work is joyless, there are so many difficult people I can't keep up. However it's much easier now I've simply labelled them all as "difficult"!'

'Charlie'

Survival Tip: Change your Posture to Change how you Feel

I've mentioned a few times how keeping a straight back when standing or sitting makes it virtually impossible to say eg 'I feel depressed' with any conviction! (Have you noticed how people only seem able to feel properly depressed when looking down? – as in 'I feel down' vs 'Things are looking up.')

'Some people make me shrink into feeling like a child, and I know I feel smaller in myself, and must look that way to others. But I've found that simply by sitting or standing straighter, I speak a little louder and look people in the eyes, and I'm an adult again, to be listened to.'

'Jack'

'I recognize the way I *physically* respond to those who press my buttons and counter with a physical response, eg changing my posture or breathing, or taking time out.'

'Andrew'

Survival Tip: **Don't Blame Yourself**

'I do not blame myself for it not working. I could always walk away. I do not need to save them from their own faults.

'Francis'

Survival Tip: **Don't Let Them Get to You**

✗ The 'enemy' may be 'giving' us a hard time, but we don't need to 'take' it on board.

Cathy's screen

'Cathy' came back after the holidays and said that she had had 'the best Christmas ever', because every time her father had started to get at her, she had allowed her very thick glass screen to rise out of the floor between them. It was thick glass, she said, so that she could see and hear everything perfectly, but – and this was the magic of it – none of his 'stuff' could get to her.

She said that they even had a joke on the next day, just the one joke, but she explained that she had never been able to stay for even one day before, let alone two.

✔ Some people I've met have chosen to have screens behind them ('People stab you in the back round here') or above them ('Have you met my bosses?!'). Others have volume controls that turn down the sound, or picture controls that make things fuzzy and 'less in your face'. One had the Berlin Wall with just a small gap to see through. Another had something like a crash helmet, very close, and padded and hard to hear through. Whatever works. Experiment. They're all the same price.

> 'I was not going to change their attitudes. I just developed a tough skin and was glad when I didn't have to deal with them any more.'
>
> *'Melissa'*

Survival Tip: Find a Way to Live with it

I was organizing a conference and discussing with a colleague how, at one point, we'd break into syndicate groups. 'I hate that word, syndicate,' I added. When he asked me why, I said it was because it was cold and mechanical to me. 'Really?' he said, 'I think of the great Chicago Mafia syndicates in the thirties, battling it out for supremacy...'. And so I'm quite happy with the word now! This process is called reframing – it's the same picture in a new frame, and can help us to put up with, or even enjoy, situations that were previously difficult.

> 'I once knew someone who was utterly brilliant and very long-winded. He insisted on finishing his sentences, even when everyone had already agreed with him and knew where he was going. Someone then told me that he was half Belgian and half Swiss, which kind of explained the behaviour to me! He wasn't being deliberately pedantic, irritating and boring. That's just how he'd been brought up, and of course I could live with that.'
>
> *'Larry'*

> 'Regarding people who seem unable to be succinct, I've sometimes backed-off from trying to hold a mirror up to their approach, in favour of just accepting it, perhaps convincing myself that that's just

easier in the long run because trying to change inherent behaviour can be very time consuming. Sometimes it's better to just learn to live with it and adapt, I think.'

'Rosemary'

Survival Tip: Focus on Just Doing a Good Job

'I've handled people best by constantly confounding them by being good at what I did and insisting on giving credit to those who helped me... '

'Melissa'

Survival Tip: Forget About *How*, for Now

There's no point in worrying about *how* you might do something, until you're crystal clear what the 'something' is. (The same applies to worrying prematurely about how you might *not* be able to do something!)

Survival Tip: Get Lots of Support and Supporters

Speak to other people: the only thing worse than feeling bullied or got at is feeling bullied or got at, and alone.

'Get someone to advocate for you. Always have a powerful fan.'

'Patricia'

'I should have asked for help earlier – not feeling I've failed if I need to ask for it – ie generally not trying to be Superwoman!'

'Victoria'

'Using my network of fabulous learning people/coaches to give me their insights has either helped me to get some objectivity or helped me realize that I wasn't on my own.'

'Nina'

'It's vital for me to take time out to explode at/with someone who is uninvolved, having asked them first; of course! And then I'll ask them to ask me some very useful questions. One of which is to ask me what would be a very good question to ask me!'

'David'

'I've handled people best by getting together with colleagues and finding ways round the limitations.'

'Charlie'

'Talk about these situations with other people, inside and outside, to get other perspectives and ideas. Especially those who are thriving in a similar situation. How exactly do they do it?'

'Edward'

'If we don't have anyone championing us, why on earth are we staying? We're not being properly looked after, organizationally. In some cases, HR will provide support but not always.'

'Francis'

Survival Tip: **Get a Coach and/or Mentor**

Or both or several – officially or informally. Ask at work. Ask your trusted aunties, uncles or friends. Tell them what role you want them to play, then use them! We have all been through tough times, and can understand if we're asked to help someone else. But be very clear, eg I want ideas, or I just want someone to listen so I can talk aloud.

You could also coach yourself:

'What could work even better is to use the techniques I employ with other people to coach myself into overcoming my weaknesses. To have a word with myself. I could also gain insight into myself by watching these relationships with similar people.'

'Keith'

Survival Tip: **Have a Deadline**

To stop a situation going on and on, set yourself a meaningful deadline, eg if it's not improved noticeably (and specify exactly what you need to notice) by 5pm on a specific date, then you will do X. And stick to it. And, most importantly, you know you can relax and not make this decision all the way up to that deadline.

Survival Tip: **If it's Not Working, Try Something Different**

'In a time of drastic change it is the learners who inherit the future. The learned usually find themselves equipped to live in a world that no longer exists.'

Eric Hoffer

Survival Tip: **It's Only Human to be Human**

We're human and want fairness, justice, closure and – let's admit it – sometimes, revenge! But because we're human we can then feel guilty, ashamed, embarrassed – and that's OK too.

It's like when people tell us not to be judgemental. Well, the only way not to be judgemental is to allow the judgement to surface (quietly, to ourselves) and then to acknowledge it (to ourselves) and put it to one side. Trying to suppress eg thoughts of revenge or guilt, simply doesn't work – they'll just keep popping up! So we acknowledge them for what they are, and then put them to one side and move on.

'I had understanding and sympathy from the organization. One guy was reprimanded and would never get much of a reference and I don't suppose he was ever able to get another job. That also gave me a bit of satisfaction, as you can guess.'

'George'

Survival Tip: **Play for Time, Play the Game**

✗ I was once in a ghastly job where it felt that everyone was against me, trying to get me out. To be honest, I realized that they were also doing this to each other, so I wasn't alone, even though it felt like it at the time. Here are some examples of what they did:

- ■ they kept changing who I and my team were to report to, fully expecting me to get angry and flounce out – but I kept explaining with a straight face that they'd had us report to so many people, why not give yet another person the experience?
- ■ they bypassed me and briefed members of my team directly – so I said that I was quite happy with that, as my team were perfectly capable and why waste time?
- ■ and the grand prize for pettiness was that I had a company car and they renewed my car tax for six months instead of a year!

✔ So I became quite adept at saying Things That Felt Right – to them, but, very importantly, to me too. I never told any lies. I never was untrue to myself. But I wanted to play for time, and the only way to do that was to play their game.

Survival Tip: **Stay Open-Minded**

It takes much less energy to stay open-minded than to keep it shut.

It works

I'm reminded here of Niels Bohr, the nuclear physicist whose visitors often remarked 'Niels, I'm surprised at you – a man of science with a lucky horseshoe above his door!' To which he twinkled 'Ah, but I'm told it works whether you believe in it or not!'

Survival Tip: **Stop Taking Yourself Literally**

We say all sorts of strange things that keep us stuck and feeling bad, eg by putting past experiences in the present tense and using metaphors of illness and discomfort. For example:

- I'm sick of this person/situation.
- My hands are tied.
- They're a real headache.
- I'm a sitting target.
- I need to keep my head down.

If we are not aware of their true meaning as we say them or think them, they can be very damaging, as we don't recognize the effect they're having on us.

✘ All of these, when I look closely at them, feel really uncomfortable to me – both mentally and physically. And that's not what we need in a difficult situation.

✔ We need to keep calm and professional, speaking (or e-mailing, or deliberately leaving a voicemail when we know they're away from their desk!) and sticking to facts, not emotions.

✔ Short sentences help. With spaces afterwards for what you've said to sink in. Bit by bit. Until you're done. Then you can say eg 'I'm done now' in order to avoid *un*doing what you've just done. And if there's an embarrassing silence, you can happily fill it. On a *different* subject. With one or more of these examples:

■ OK, so the next item is X.
■ Thanks for listening.
■ I'll wait for you to respond to me.
■ I obviously want us to get this right, this time, by being fully briefed.

Survival Tip: Take Responsibility vs Blaming Others

Let's just stop and ask ourself if we are 100 per cent the victim in this 'enemy' situation, or was it perhaps our fault in some tiny little way, either starting the situation off, or helping it to continue or get worse? None of these questions is particularly useful, of course, compared to 'Am I prepared to take responsibility to fix it and acknowledge that I obviously played *some* part in it, but this is about the future, not blaming the past?' Without taking responsibility, we're just going to be looking to blame others, and there's no forward movement possible that way, is there?

Survival Tip: Take the Controls Instead of Looking like a Victim

Think of this as an 'enemy' situation that you *can* do something about, rather than an 'enemy' person who's beyond your control.

'Make them feel safe and remind yourself that you have no need of them. Smile and be happy and do brilliant work.'

'Virginia'

Survival Tip: **Thoughts vs Feelings – the Great Self-Destructive Battleground**

You may find this hard to believe but I absolutely promise you that no one in the history of this planet (including you and me) has ever truly:

- *felt* like killing someone; or
- *felt* like they were under attack; or
- *felt* that someone was putting pressure on them.

That's because if there's a 'that' or a 'like' then the 'feeling' is really a thought.
   But, I hear you say, we so often see and hear people acting out their 'feelings', such as:

- I feel angry.
- They made me feel small.
- I felt disrespected.
- I feel stupid when I'm with them.

Indeed, these can be so all-consuming that in extreme cases they can even be used to sum up an entire person, for example:

- He/she is such an angry person.
- I'm insignificant.
- I'm not worthy of any respect from anyone.
- I'm stupid.

But – thank goodness – even though these can 'feel' devastating, all of these are 'thinkings', not feelings. They happen in our mind, not in our body, and so, thank goodness, it's relatively easy to change our mind.
   Here's how this happens. True feelings are literal and descriptive bodily sensations, *with no interpretation put onto them*, for example:

- ■ hot, cold;
- ■ tense, relaxed;
- ■ spinning, dizzy;
- ■ shaking, shivering;
- ■ sharp pain, dull ache, pressure.

So when we say we're feeling angry or stupid, for example, we might actually be interpreting sensations such as 'hot and shaking and tensed up', or 'tight and cold and rigid'. And most of these sensations actually last for well under one minute.

'What?!' I hear you saying, 'but I know people who've been angry or sad for days or weeks or months or years.' And you're right, but they've been angry or sad, by *thinking* angry or sad. It's like this:

1. something happens (eg we notice or realize something, or someone says or does something);
2. our body responds with chemicals which rush around our body, making it impossible to think clearly at the same time;
3. but nevertheless, we try to think clearly! About, for example:
   - the event; and
   - how we are feeling because of the chemicals; and
   - what we plan to do next; and
   - what we're fearing, based on the past.
4. and our thoughts produce their own chemical reactions;
5. and so it goes on, in self-perpetuating circles.

For example, speaking personally, something might happen to 'make me feel angry' (ie cause me to tighten in my chest, tense my jaw, get really hot and start shaking). But my mind starts thinking about:

- ■ How dare they!
- ■ I'm going to show them, once and for all...
- ■ But I don't want to make a fuss...
- ■ So I'm really trapped...

■ But I don't want to end up working late again...
■ But I don't see any choice...
■ How dare they! (Again!!)

And it's – you will have guessed by now – largely *my thoughts of revenge* that keep me 'feeling' angry. No one actually 'makes me' 'feel angry'. It's me all by myself. And this is why we make little sense when we're eg angry. There's such a muddle of thoughts and chemicals, it's almost impossible for anyone to make sense of it.

> 'Getting cross didn't work – he just found it amusing!'
>
> *'Harry'*

Survival Tip: **Treat Yourself**

Quite simply, if we've been having a tough time, maybe we can also have a little good time, eg a nice walk or...

> 'Chocolate, booze... tranquilizers?!' (Just joking, I think.)
>
> *'Sheila'*

Survival Tip: **Trust Your Instincts**

Our instincts are what we might call 'something told me this wasn't the right thing to do' or 'I had a funny feeling at the time that this wouldn't work out well,' and as an early warning system they're invaluable as an input to balance all this corporate 'We should...', 'You must...' stuff.

> 'I need to be brave, listen to my intuition and act fairly swiftly on it.'
>
> *'Harry'*

> 'I'm well-advised to go with my gut instincts about things that worry me, and react quickly, rather than rationalizing it out and hoping it will go away. I have to live with me, not with these other people.'
>
> *'Rochelle'*

'Don't play the game or collude with the bitching or whatever it happens to be – push back responsibility to those who own it, eg not giving feedback on behalf of others, not hearing feedback about someone again and again whilst being asked not to say anything.'

'David'

Survival Tip: Turn Goliath into David

✗ We can monsterize people and situations in our mind's eye so that they loom large, and we feel small as a consequence.

✗ If you think now of an 'enemy' I bet you can see or feel them looming large, or hear them at their most destructive, in your mind's eye.

✔ Try shrinking them down to size and put this picture among a gallery of other people. Have the 'enemies' in black and white, small and without sound, on your left. And have the friends in colour and in nice frames with nice sounds, to your right and in front of you.

✔ Remember that they're all human beings and all of them can both 'behave' and 'misbehave'. It's the *behaviour* of the person in the picture frame we need to deal with. That's all.

Part 2

The Fifteen Toughest Types of 'Enemy', with Survive and Thrive Strategies

What all 'enemy' situations have in common is that we feel bad, and find it hard to think clearly, and so what all of these 'types' have in common is that they are easy to recognize by the effect that they have upon *us*.

If you need a reference book for handling *specific* types of behaviour in other people, then the companion volume *How People Tick* (also by Mike Leibling and published by Kogan Page) has over 50 types detailed, with tips for handling them, eg Angry People, Boring People, Competitive People.

> 'There is one common denominator to all my most difficult people – they don't see themselves as difficult no matter how offensive they are or to how many people.'
>
> *'Virginia'*

You may find that some 'really difficult' people appear under more than one 'type' (surprise, surprise!). The headings are to help identify who we're dealing with, and which Survive and Thrive Strategies are particularly pertinent. But check out again the Essential Survival Strategies and Tips in Part 1 and the Action Tips in Part 4, if you can't wait, for any ideas that are worth a try. As they say, 'A good idea doesn't mind who has it!'

11

Type 1:
People Who Bully

Bullies use power inappropriately, as they think they can pull your strings or cut your strings and expect you to string along, and look up to them. That's why I much prefer the term 'puppeteer' to 'bully' because it describes more clearly what they are trying to do, and because our solution is clear – the strings must be disconnected somehow. Moreover, it is much more empowering to think of oneself as a puppet (with a potentially large selection of scissors) than as a victim, yes?

'They are not being honest – I've been hearing that they're saying stuff about me to others but not to my face.'

'Larry'

'Those that magically make you feel small, insignificant and worthless by attacking you at an identity level and/or not respecting your values.'

'Virginia'

'Mrs Charisma, who you need to impress, throwing you off balance by asking "And what do you do?" in that tone that implies that it won't be anything remotely interesting or worthy – this tends to throw you (me) off balance and you look like a fish out of water, a lot of mouth opening and closing with not much coming out! This is when having a few well-rehearsed lines comes in useful, something to fall back on.'

''Patricia'

'People in positions of power who deliberately use intimidation don't engage and involve others (authoritarian style) or indeed tell you to do a big involved and complex piece of work with no ideas, support, proposals, guidelines, then when you present it, say they don't like it, it's not what they want and either own it themselves as their brilliant piece of work or drop it entirely and move on to something else.'

'Melissa'

'Confidence crushers. People who "make us" feel small, unsure of ourselves.'

'Edward'

'Meeting your new boss for the first time and she announces to you that she thinks you have significant skills gaps' (difficult to recover from that one).

'Pamela'

'Not having the same qualifications as everyone else and being constantly reminded of the fact.'

'Charlie'

'People who bully, limit others' aspirations, stereotype, take credit for others' work or don't give credit where it's due, who don't recognize differing perspectives, who play politics behind the scenes in ways that benefit them but don't help the people they're there to serve.'

'Rochelle'

'People being unnecessarily spiteful, unkind and even using bullying tactics to get what they want – it's not right, necessary or useful, it demotivates and creates total fear, then has the expected effect on people not doing well – being confused, not reaching potential or feeling good – no feedforward, only unhelpful useless negative feedback.'

'David'

'People who are being difficult for the sake of being difficult because they think it's clever and it unsettles people – different values to mine.'

'Natalie'

Survive and Thrive Strategies

■ We always have choices. They may not be immediately obvious (otherwise we wouldn't hear so often 'I wish I thought of that earlier'), so take a little time to think.

■ We obviously, ultimately, need to cut the strings or get someone else to help, or to do it for us.

■ See other tips on Bullying, pages 39–45.

12

Type 2:
People Who Put their own Needs First

Some people seem unable to work with shared agendas and have hidden or multiple or selfish agendas and come across, therefore, as manipulative.

'People whose decisions and beliefs may be motivated by personal advancement or political gain as opposed to the greater good. They are disloyal and untrustworthy, saying one thing to your face and another behind your back. They can be bullies too. For example, when someone runs a session that they label as "consultative", but it becomes apparent that there is no flexibility, or room for change. Uncollaborative approach to working. Not showing empathy.'

'Virginia'

'They make the worst possible decisions because they are based on the decision's impact on themselves, and not on the project or corporation as a whole.'

'Larry'

'Too occupied by needing to be recognized themselves, which clouds their awareness of others and their impact on them.'

'Patricia'

'People who are political (they have a hidden agenda that makes me feel manipulated).'

'Rosemary'

Survive and Thrive Strategies

■ On the one hand we need to recognize that virtually everyone has their own personal agenda (eg to be seen to be worthy of promotion) as well as their professional task-related agendas. These often get muddled, as seen above, unless there's a clear path for exploring them, and that should be the regular meetings we have with our boss (at least once a month) and our regular appraisals (at least once every six months – a year is too long to wait).

■ Appraisals are where *both* sides appraise each other of progress against previous goals, and where new goals are set for *both* parties, eg I shall train two new colleagues, and you in return will reduce my workload by 25 per cent so that I can do this. We should set out what exactly we want to achieve, and what help we'll need in getting there. Our monthly meetings should be about how *we're* doing, and what tweaks might be needed to help us to get there. They are about *us*, not about projects. They are about *how* we do our work, not about the work itself. (That's what progress meetings are for.)

■ It's very likely that people with hidden agendas haven't had clear appraisals with *their* boss. So it may be useful to chat with them sometime about *their* goals and dreams, and how they are getting on with them, and how you're happy to help if they like, so at least they can talk to you if not to *their* boss. After all, they're human too. And, by requesting regular monthly meetings and six-monthly appraisals for yourself (with written agendas, please, for focus), you can demonstrate how much you value them, and encourage your boss to get the same value from their boss.

13

Type 3:
People Who are Hard
to Connect with

Maybe they don't listen or cannot or will not make a decision or they seem to be on a different wavelength or planet. Hard as we try we just don't seem to understand them or get through to them.

'I had a member of my team who never seemed to be quite there and although bright and able was incredibly difficult to manage. I did try various managing strategies but nothing worked until I sat down and had a really gloves-off chat and it transpired that he was in the position of looking through a window at everything, ie he was not associated into any experience he had. Things evolved from there, but I guess the point is that in virtually all cases people are not doing this "difficult" stuff on purpose. He so didn't know he was doing it and when he did know, he hadn't a clue why.'

'Andrew'

'How can we debate with someone who can come across as stubborn or immovable and who won't debate because they can't debate? On the surface it might seem as if they won't listen to reason as they have very entrenched beliefs or preconceived ideas – possibly inherited from other people and not always based on the available evidence (that is obvious to everyone except them, it seems). So they stick to their guns, they bully, they hammer away "their" opinions and point of view. Or, since they don't have any real opinions of their own, they can do the opposite and change their mind on a whim often without being able or prepared to explain why.'

'Jack'

'People who are defended by another person, ie shielded, protected for whatever reason and who interpret any comment/offer of support/suggestion for how something could be done differently as criticism.'

'Rochelle'

'People who are very closed and guarded can feel like hard work.'

'Larry'

'More-than-my-job's-worth types, ie local government, traffic wardens!'

'Victoria'

'People at call centres of banks, telecommunications companies and computer software/program companies who tell you that something cannot be done, or is not allowed. This is mostly because they don't have the training or information to help and don't know how to get it.'

'Nina'

'Those with completely closed minds and possibly not enough confidence in themselves.'

'David'

'People who don't have a mind of their own and so they defend to the hilt "their" second-hand beliefs.'

'Charlie'

Survive and Thrive Strategies

■ Ask them. What do I need to do to communicate more effectively with you? What do I need to do to help you feel more comfortable with me?

■ Put things in writing, but send them to yourself first. Ask yourself whether it's crystal clear what exactly you're asking of them.

14

Type 4:
People Who are
Out of their Depth

This is a difficult category to handle, because they are on thin ice and know it. They may be in a fragile situation personally, emotionally, professionally, or in every area of their life. For example, I met someone who'd been divorced and was still hurting enormously. They'd been told to come on this course I was running, but it was obvious that they were so occupied by what was going on in their head, that they would find it really hard to take in anything new, let alone risk upsetting their fragile state of mind. (They sat very close to the exit, with their coat on, clutching the chair with both hands, looking terrified.) I went over and said that I was very pleased that they'd come and that many people just come and go as they like, and that was fine, to do what they felt was right for them. She looked immensely relieved, and fled, very sensibly I thought.

When someone's just about managing to keep their head above water, even the slightest ripple can cause drowning.

'This was an extreme circumstance – but I knew a set of parents unable to accept that their son had special needs. They were possibly afraid of consequent marriage difficulties not only for them but for their other children.'

'Victoria'

'There have been times when people have taken something that I said too seriously and it has made them worse than if I had left them alone. For example, when I have said to nervous or shy people to spread your wings a little they take it as if I had told them to become so over-confident that they end up badly humiliating themselves.'

'Nina'

'People who are incompetent in positions of authority are the worst. My present boss is not as bad as he might be, but insecure and talks over people.'

'Charlie'

'I've come across people who think/behave as if they are experts in everyone else's field and approach every question in the sure and certain knowledge that there's nothing they don't know. It causes problems, to say the least, when they are dealing with areas about which they know nothing!'

'Rochelle'

'People who can't make decisions, can't communicate what they expect. Don't have or can't seem to articulate clear objectives, ramble on, don't get to the point; don't have any idea of what they want, and then when you present options say that's not what they wanted and make you feel stupid, because you can't read their minds or crystal-ball gaze (when they obviously don't know what they want).'

'Edward'

'Those who shift problems onto others and if things don't work out always blame someone else. In its extreme form, people who will cry discrimination/accuse colleagues of all sorts of prejudice and unfairness, rather than accept any responsibility themselves for how things work out.'

'Larry'

'Managers who delegate work (as a work-avoidance strategy). I tend to take up new interesting assignments with relish. This, however, seriously backfired when I did such a good job on Project A that I was heaped with fulsome praise in public by the CEO. Result: my line manager did not speak to me for several weeks.'

'Rosemary'

Survive and Thrive Strategies

- ■ Avoid pushing them further out of their depth.
- ■ Ask as little of them as possible.
- ■ Let them know they're not alone by offering friendship even at the basic level of just saying 'Hello' (and not pushing them into feeling they need to have conversations by asking scary – to them – questions like 'How are you?').
- ■ Maybe suggest that they get support from eg their doctor or an employee assistance programme and – without forcing them to do so – offer to go with them, if they like.
- ■ But if in doubt it's best advised to leave well alone, especially if the consequences could be widespread and beyond our expertise and influence. After all, we're colleagues, not counsellors.

15

Type 5:
People Who Meddle

There are, I believe, only three genuinely worthwhile roles/functions/jobs in most organizations:

- serving customers (internal or external);
- supporting those who are serving customers;
- directing the organization in terms of viability and direction.

The last thing any of us needs is a confusion of roles. I simplify somewhat, but in essence we need to know:

- who is at the front line;
- who is supporting them;
- and that someone's looking after the direction of the whole organization, while everyone else is getting on with business, so to speak.

Nothing else. And this is as true of big corporations as it is of small schools and everything in between. That's why we need managers to manage the *shape* of what we do, leaving us to do the doing:

'They can feel very controlling – they think they're delegating but constantly check up on you so you wonder why they don't just do it themselves! Takes any fun/originality/stretch out of it.'

'Larry'

'Most big jobs run over budget and are over-staffed due to the inability of key players to stand back and let the job be done by the most competent people even if, horrors, the job would not be as the micromanager would do it.'

'Sheila'

'The managers who review every stick of stationery, phone calls etc and require documentation of every usage.'

'Harry'

'White-anters – an Australian term for undermining a project or person. White-anting is a phrase used to describe the process of undermining something, or eating away at something below the surface. Just as white ants eat away at the core of a tree or piece of timber without disturbing the surface, so too can senior managers eat away at the heart of a project without their actions being noticed on the surface. In fact, their actions can go entirely unnoticed until the whole project caves in.'

'Brian'

Survive and Thrive Strategies

■ I would always calmly point out the dilemma I'm in and ask them to resolve it for me.

'I would point out that on the one hand you've asked me to do this, and on the other hand you're stopping me doing this the way I know how. Help me out please, what exactly do you want me to do, and by when? Please leave me to do it the way I know how. I promise I'll come and ask for help if needs be. Anything else?'

'Keith'

16

Type 6:
People Who are Fickle

When we don't know where we are or stand, essentially there is a lack of boundaries to ensure acceptable, reasonably consistent, and reasonably predictable behaviour.

'People who change their minds on a whim, or appear to, often without being able or prepared to explain why.'

'Charlie'

'They keep changing the goal posts – they say they want one thing but when you go back to them with that one thing, say they wanted something else or, even worse, saying that they never asked for that thing in the first place!'

'Francis'

'Those who say one thing and do another – the inconsistent and the charming non-deliverer.'

'Sheila'

'The obtuse, those who say they understand what you have just communicated, agree that it has been made clear and then go on to swiftly prove that either they didn't or they've chosen to ignore you.'

'Rosemary'

'People who are unreliable or blow hot and cold about things, or promise everything but don't deliver and let other people down. This may of course indicate my incompetence in dealing with them rather than their inconsistency (or indeed my control freakery in wanting everything to work out according to plan!). Often these have been people who can be charming with flashes of brilliance, but others who know them have tended to say the same – "She's a lovely person and can be fantastic to work with, but she drives me mad because... ". A variant of this is the senior person who goes about being charismatic and distributing largesse, which partner agencies/audiences think is wonderful – but who relies on an army of minions running along behind making it happen – or worse, having to explain diplomatically why it can't actually happen...! This is the person who has quadruple-booked himself (I'm sorry but in my experience it is himself!) but doesn't notice until 10 minutes before the appointments are due, and then just assumes you'll just drop everything to cover something vital at the other end of the city/country... '

'Brian'

'Inconsistency – where behaviour and performance are erratic, sometimes very good and sometimes very low. Moodiness resulting in people not knowing where they are or what to expect. People who you agree deadlines or timescales with and you still need to chase them. Finally, the completely disorganized. However nice they are, it inevitably affects other people's planning, provides for ludicrous (and usually missed before you know about them) deadlines and results in a string of things that are unfinished. What I did was ignore it and do my own thing. That can have advantages in autonomy, but it can also hold things up and cause missed chances. In retrospect, I could have tried to organize her a bit more – eg by sending agendas ahead of meetings etc. (However, she wouldn't have read them!) Was also affected by being hugely understaffed myself because she wasn't getting me the resources I was repeatedly asking for. Going over her head was the only other option and I had been expressly told not to do that and followed suit out of loyalty.'

'Keith'

Survive and Thrive Strategies

■ Put as much as possible in writing (and if necessary explain that it's to help you to focus). Review it with them.

■ Ensure that you send very clear messages (to help them with their boundaries) but consider a light humorous touch. (I remember a very pompous memo from a new finance director being sent back to him with a scribbled note saying 'Pat, you need to know that someone's been writing pompous memos and signing your name at the bottom.' There were no more pompous memos.)

■ Ensure they are not dumping on you, see pages 43–45.

17

Type 7: People Who are Unlike Me

Some people's values or ways of working or communicating can be just so different to ours! If we think of a piano keyboard, some people play irritatingly high notes. Others boom out ponderously low notes, whereas we – of course – play perfectly in the middle! But it's useful to use the whole keyboard, unless we only want to get on with people who are just like us, isn't it?

For example, I knew someone who spoke REALLY LOUDLY ALL THE TIME, whereas I am quietly spoken (most of the time) and loudness physically hurts my ears. I used to try talking quietly, to encourage him to do the same. But it just succeeded in having him talk louder and louder. Until I realized that if I got a little louder myself (ie moved towards his place on the keyboard) then he would be able to hear me more comfortably. And after a short while, if I got softer again, so did he. So maybe if we could tell the other person, somehow, or lead them by example, or else...

'I find I have to try to use his words and thought patterns. The other thing is he is lazy, funnily enough – so if you can get into parallel with his way of thinking you don't have to do much to impress him. God, this is sickening to read, I am sure.'

'Patricia'

'I was in a taxi once, and the driver started with "I'm not racist, but...", and regaled me with racist attitudes for the whole journey. I have never felt so uncomfortable, and had we not been in the middle of a large rural expanse, I would certainly have got out and walked. I could feel myself getting more and more twisted inside, until I pretended to feel nauseous. That stopped him, as no taxi driver wants to risk their taxi being out of service for cleaning. But his attitude literally did make me feel sick.'

'Larry'

'There was a manically driven control freak (and bully) that I once had the misfortune to work for. Her controlling overran into dictating ahead of time what everyone had to say in every forum, whether she was there or not. She gave me a complex about public speaking that I still have. She also thought that 'managing people out' was a viable course of action and expected me to take part in victimizing people (which I didn't, although I'm afraid I didn't stand up for them either).'

'Melissa'

Survive and Thrive Strategies

■ See some common differences in *how* we communicate (ie fail to communicate!) in the questions 'Know Your Enemy' in Part 3, page 132 and talk *their* language if you want to get through to them more clearly.

■ Ask them how they would prefer you to work together – put aside some time to discuss *how* you could work better together, rather than *what* you're both working on.

18

Type 8:
People Who are
Like Me

'For me, the most difficult people I've found to work with are those most like myself. When someone has the same strengths and weaknesses, our strengths sometimes clash and our weaknesses amplify each other. If I can't deal with weaknesses in myself, it is even more difficult to deal with them in other people.'

'Pamela'

Survive and Thrive Strategies

- We need to recognize when we are both in danger of trying to occupy the same space, and agree not to tread on each other's toes by discussing how we can best work together, eg I'd love it if you could do/say/stop doing/saying X.
- We maybe need to be working further apart, on different areas or projects.
- We maybe need to develop a friendship outside work so that we can enjoy our similarities, and focus on the work itself during working hours.

19

Type 9:
People Who are
Close to Me

It can be harder to handle people who are close to us, as we can't just walk away from the situation if we want to maintain our friendship as well as our working relationship. One of the two has to suffer, and resentment can follow.

> 'I constantly amaze myself that the closer people are to me the worse I can be at handling them.'
>
> *'Virginia'*

Survive and Thrive Strategies

If two people who are close to each other are working together, they might:

■ keep to strict boundaries, eg agreeing that at work there will be no private conversations whatsoever, including at break times (this can be very excluding for colleagues, in any case);

■ agree that outside work (eg when at home or travelling together) they will have no conversations that should be covered in the workplace (and get someone else with whom they can 'offload' their work concerns);

■ consider calling each other by different names, eg Fred at work and Frederick at home;

■ think about one of them moving to work in a different location if the above doesn't work out;

■ enquire about any policies that their organization might have, so they know where they both stand.

20

Type 10:
Me Myself

Many of us find that we can suffer from our *own* actions.

'Sometimes I know I can be my own worst enemy. I need a friend or colleague to warn me early on.'

'Melissa'

Of course we don't deliberately cause ourselves problems, but things don't always turn out as planned. Either because it's simply not that easy to predict exactly *what* will happen in the future, or because it's hard to get an objective perspective on 'me' and *how* I am doing things, especially while I'm concentrating on doing them.

Indeed, when talking with other people I'm sure we all hear 'But it's so obvious now: why on earth couldn't I see that myself?' and the answer is simple; that we are in the middle of our situation whereas other people are outside it. We all, therefore, simply have different perspectives. Other people can move around the situation, whereas we have been in one place, inside it. And, quite naturally, people in different places will see different things and draw different conclusions.

Survive and Thrive Strategies

■ We should always talk to other people to get different perspectives, and to build a three-dimensional view of the situation instead of a one-dimensional view.

■ If we've been focusing on satisfying other people's needs, then we might have lost track of what our own needs are – and, therefore, felt like the loser. And so we might need to express our own needs, eg 'I really appreciate all the extra work/experience you've been offering me but right now I need to get my life more into balance and spend my evenings and weekends with my family and friends, thank you.'

■ Satisfying needs is like giving to charity and, like charity, it 'begins at home'. (And surely we should pay our needs at least the same attention as we pay others' – after all, who else will do it for us?)

■ If and when we get things 'wrong' – and remember, we only find this out *after* the event – we need not be hard on ourselves. It's not that 'I'm an idiot' or 'I'm always messing things up' or 'I'm my own worst enemy (again?),' it's simply that 'I'm not a clairvoyant!' and 'Nobody knows everything' and 'If people had to make sure everything was perfect, nothing would ever get done.'

21

Type 11:
Everybody Else

When it seems like everybody is against us, or is on a different wavelength or comes from a different planet, then it's desperately exhausting and lonely because there's little chance that we can change a whole organization. After all, every organization has its own personality and attracts like-minded people. And we can't change all of them, realistically, can we?

Survive and Thrive Strategies

■ If we can't afford to get out financially, then we can at least get out emotionally by focusing on doing a crisply professional job, not taking things personally, and finding our next job.

■ We need to recognize that the three key factors of a satisfactory relationship with an organization are that we should:
  – like it;
  – trust it; and
  – respect it.

It's the same three features that are ideal in a boss (or, indeed, in a partner and in many other relationships). But when one or more of these is missing, and it's unlikely to change, how long do we need to wait to be convinced?

■ We need to *try* to find a like-minded colleague (and maybe there truly aren't any). Is there *anyone* around who also seems not to be part of a clique or gang who you might get to know? At least you might support each other.

■ Admit to your mistakes. I once worked in a company where I should have left within a few minutes of joining. It felt toxic, and indeed *was* toxic – for me. In a different context, it's like if we're not enjoying a party, then the simple truth is that it's not the right party for us (whether time-wise, mood-wise, people-wise or everything-wise), and we should simply leave.

■ Maybe check your job description or specification or the person specification: now that you know what the job and the place are like, were they accurate? If not, then it's perfectly acceptable to tell your boss, or HR, that in your opinion the job is not what you were led to expect, and that trying to force yourself to fit in, or to force the organization to accommodate you, isn't going to work. And then – and this is the important bit – ask to negotiate a severance package. You want to get out anyway. Why should you (literally) pay for their mistake?

■ See Action Tip – Getting out may truly be your best option, page 167.

22

Type 12:
People Who Regard Me as a Type, Not a Person

Stereotyping can be really offensive, but as a shorthand, it enables us to cut many corners, eg we know it's not a good idea to shout at someone who we want to help us, or we try to avoid slang with someone whose first language is different from ours. But sometimes it's meant very personally.

> 'There was that creative team in the advertising agency telling me that I couldn't possibly work on beer as how would women know anything about beer.'
>
> *'Rochelle'*

> 'Secretaries who have the idea that because you are female, then as they are also female, there is no part of your job that they are not up to doing – even if you have a couple of degrees and 20-plus years' experience in your field compared to their three years of high school.'
>
> *'Sheila'*

> 'The Great White Male. The manager who decides you can't have a promotion or raise because you have a family, and there have been instances where you chose to take time for the family over overtime on the job. Males who are convinced that because you are female you are automatically a lower form of life, and therefore, even if they

are officially reporting to you, they don't have to, and can report to any male in the office. Males who assume that because you are female that you got the job you currently hold because of either family influence, sleeping with someone up the corporate ladder, or as a result of affirmative action, or all three.'

'Sheila'

Survive and Thrive Strategies

■ Don't take it personally – take it behaviourally and state the obvious, eg 'Yes, I'm a woman and yes, many women know nothing about beer, but many women are able to be objective and open-minded unlike many men, I suppose, so shall we get on with the task in hand, [and this bit is optional] boys?' or 'You seem to think you can do my job, and so let's think about giving you some projects to see how you get on with them, what do you think? Let me know, please.'

23

Type 13:
People Who
'Change' Me

'People who make me feel small.'

'Melissa'

'The people I find hardest to deal with are those whose presence changes me – so it's dealing with me in response to others that is the issue.'

'Francis'

'Another difficult person who is the one who tries to change you, especially when they try to make you like them'

'Susannah'

Survive and Thrive Strategies

■ Let's not kid ourselves. No-one can change us, or make us feel eg small. *They* might do X and then *we* might do Y and, yes, it might have happened time and time again, but no-one *makes* us respond in this way, as long as we have a goal in mind, eg feel calm, think professional.

'I used to find myself feeling like a little child when my boss used to shout at me in meetings, like being told off by a parent or teacher.

Then one day someone asked me how long I was going to let him affect me this way. I decided there and then to have a bunch of very grown-up statements that would make my point firmly, and not play the quivering wreck any more. So "Maybe we can talk about this calmly when you're not so emotional?" and "Let's keep this professional, Pat. My opinion is… " were my two favourites to use. But in the event I found that I just needed to think these statements, and a calm look towards Pat did more to help him realize that he was acting like a child having a tantrum! I followed up with a solicitous "Are you OK?" in private later, and felt that I'd taken control of the situation, which I suppose, looking back, I had.'

'Pamela'

24

Type 14:
People Who Bring out
the Rescuer in Me

'The reason they stick to me is because I stick around helping them. They don't know the answer to their own problems or behaviour and like a magnet I am attracted to them to help, possibly because I see solutions and I seem to like solving things and I find them interesting. Unfortunately, once I have understood them they are often not that interesting and I can't get away from them; they now need me, having never had so much attention. Which is probably the under-lying behaviour in me, not them.'

'Tamatha'

Survive and Thrive Strategies

- As soon as we feel the slightest urge to solve others' prob-lems and get sucked in, we need to remember that we need to help them to fix their own situation – with our support, of course.
- We need to ask them questions that will guide them to think for themselves, eg 'What have you considered doing so far?' 'What have you already tried?' 'What do you think might be a good way of approaching this?' 'How would it be if you thought this through first and then tell me what you think?'

25

Type 15:
People Who Bring out the Rebel in Me, the Worst in Me

'I suppose it is down to my upbringing and my family's needs that I really have trouble with authoritarian figures. Whether in a business or bureaucratic context, I find myself seething when all logic, reason and (to me) obvious solutions are brushed aside and nothing, but nothing, will shift the They're-My-Rules-And-Nothing-Else-Goes mindset.'

'Sheila'

Survive and Thrive Strategies

■ Because I find it impossible not to retaliate (and yet I realize that this would be unproductive!) I do it internally. I imagine shouting at them (internally) and then when I'm done, I become beautifully professional in my response. (After all, it's my problem, not theirs.)

Part 3

Getting New Information for New Ways of Moving Forward

INTRODUCTION

There is a tendency in organizations (including families and friends) to feel that we 'should' leap into action and do something rather than think it through carefully, and then prepare plans and possibilities.

This section will help you get as much information as possible before embarking on your decision planning. After all, why would anyone start to action something as important as resolving an 'enemy' situation without gathering and processing all the information and intelligence that there is, or rush into action based on inadequate data?

This is not a rhetorical question, so to answer it maybe:

- we couldn't bear to think about it;
- we thought it was best to keep our head down;

■ we were so scared/depressed etc that we couldn't think clearly;
■ we didn't want to admit it to anyone else (or to ourselves);
■ we succumbed to pressure, and didn't act on our instincts and experience.

All of these are perfectly common but by comprehensive information gathering we can hopefully pre-empt comments like these below, that we frequently hear once a situation *has* been resolved:

■ Why on earth didn't I do that earlier?
■ How come I couldn't see that myself?
■ If only I'd realized that before!
■ So that's why nothing I did actually had the desired effect!

'Life is lived forwards but understood backwards.'

Søren Kierkegaard

This section in *Working with the Enemy* offers, therefore, many ways of gathering information prior to processing it into a plan. After all, if we had had sufficient information, and a clear step-by-step process when we had tried (and tried and tried) to do something about the situation before, we might well have been able to see the wood for the trees. And until we are sufficiently informed on a problem, how can we start to try and fix it?

'...the detectives...don't seem at all able to see the solution' said Staines. 'It isn't that they can't see the solution. It is that they can't see the problem,' said Father Brown.

(from *The Point of a Pin*, by G K Chesterton).

26

Top Tips for Information Gathering

1. Remember, this is information gathering, not beating yourself up (again) for not having fixed the situation. If you begin to feel negative emotions, sit up *very* straight or stand up *very* straight, as it's very hard to feel 'low' when doing this. (I bet you've never seen anyone with a straight back saying 'I feel depressed'!)

2. So even though you're looking at and into your own situation, think of yourself as a journalist, gathering information, data, perspectives etc about a situation that *has* existed, in the past (maybe many times).

3. And remember that you need to gather as much information as possible in order to create an improved situation in the future. And the best way of doing this is not to relive the ghastly feelings that were involved at the time, but to coolly spot the patterns at play, with the wonderful freedom of not needing to make any decisions yet. Harvest first and then you can decide strategies and actions later based on what you've harvested.

4. You do *not* need to make any decisions whatsoever at this stage; your job is simply to consider deeply and write, write, write.

5. If some of these questions seem hard, that's only natural, isn't it?
6. Please sit or stand upright with your head up, to help you to separate clearly:
   - the information (which you want to keep and learn from); and
   - the emotions (which you want to keep in the past where they belong).
7. Please note that all information should be written in the *past tense*, because:
   ✔ the events happened in the past;
   ✔ the emotions belonged to these past events;
   ✘ the (negative) emotions don't need to be experienced ever again in the present or in the future, do they?
8. Inadequate data lead to inadequate decisions, so please write down every single thing that comes to mind, however trivial, obvious or weird it might seem. Remember that great journalists always keep their objectivity and just ask great thought-provoking questions, and record the answers. They don't judge, as that stops the flow.
9. And just like journalists do, you can return to consider some of these questions time and time again – there are no prizes for speed here.
10. Please fill them in, in the order they're presented, as the sequence is important to develop your thinking.
11. But ignore the order they're in, and fill in what you can, then return to the others, if you prefer!
12. A great question works as an 'invitation to consider', ie to think deeply. So here are some invitations to get you considering – ie thinking deeply – in new ways and in new areas, to get as much information as you possibly can.
13. But, I repeat, you do not need to think about doing anything with the information yet.
14. And when you've gone through the whole section, writing notes in the margin, start again at the beginning and this time concentrate on:

- areas that you've not considered much up to now, where it could be rewarding to harvest more learnings; or
- where you've been so satisfied with the first information that emerged, that you've not yet challenged yourself to dig deeper.

27

Information Questionnaire

1. THE SITUATION

ⓘ What has made the situation better (even if only a little and/or for a short time)?

ⓘ What has made the situation worse (even if only a little and/or for a short time)?

ⓘ What has made the situation no better or worse (even if only a little and/or for a short time)?

ⓘ In a year's time will the situation be better or worse or stay the same, if you don't do anything?

ⓘ So what must you avoid to ensure it doesn't get worse?

ⓘ And how *might* you be able to make the situation at least stay the same, or even get better?

2. THE ENEMY

Here are some common types of 'enemy' – what type(s) would you say that yours has been? (And jot down any others, too.)

ⓘ An attention-seeking playground bully who needs an audience?

ⓘ A quiet, in private, intruder who doesn't want public attention?

ⓘ The pretend friend, duplicitous, double or triple agent, who says 'trust me'?

ⓘ A behind your back, underhand, not to your face, rumour monger?

ⓘ Acting out of personal jealousy, eg jealous of your popularity?

ⓘ Acting out of professional jealousy, eg jealous of your position or skills?

ⓘ Setting you up to fail with unreasonable targets or requests?

ⓘ Originally playful, joking and friendly but things turned sour when they 'went too far'?

ⓘ Different values to you, eg using insulting, suggestive, racist or otherwise inappropriate (for you) language?

ⓘ Maybe like this to some extent because of something you yourself might have said or done, even way back?

ⓘ Maybe, you suspect, unwitting and blind to the effects of their actions?

3. KNOW YOUR ENEMY

Let's see where you are or are not 'on the same wavelength' in terms of *how* you have been communicating.

Visual? Auditory? Kinaesthetic? Digital?

ⓘ Are they predominantly *visual*, using phrases such as 'Do you see what I mean?' 'Get the picture?'

ⓘ Or are they predominantly *auditory*, using phrases such as 'Do you hear what I say?' 'Does this sound right to you?'

ⓘ Or are they predominantly *kinaesthetic*, using phrases such as 'Does this grab you?' 'Do you get what I mean?' 'Let's push ahead, move along.'

ⓘ Or are they predominantly *digital*, using none of the above seeing/hearing/doing phrases but talking like politicians and saying little! For example 'There's a reason why things are as they are' or 'It's important that we all know we're strategic.'
ⓘ And you?

Judging?

ⓘ Do they predominantly judge *externally*, ie by what other people have written, said or researched?
ⓘ Do they predominantly judge *internally*, ie by what they themselves feel?
ⓘ And you?

What number?

I have a friend who shouted at his daughter 'How many times do I have to tell you to get ready for school?!' to which he got the calm reply 'Four, Daddy.' Once he got over his surprise, he realized that she never did *anything* until asked or told four times. Result: he kept calm, knowing that shouting would make no difference.

ⓘ So, does the 'enemy' predominantly judge on just one exposure to evidence or feelings, or how many times do they need?
ⓘ And you?

Positive or negative?

ⓘ Do they tend to talk about what they like or what they want?

ⓘ Or do they tend to talk more about what they dislike or what's wrong?

ⓘ And you?

Detail or big picture?

ⓘ Are they particularly meticulous, detailed or fussy?

ⓘ Or are they more 'big picture' and 'Don't bother me with the details'?

ⓘ And you?

First, second or third person?

Do you remember from school that:

■ First person = me;
■ Second person = you;
■ Third person = them.

So:

ⓘ Are they more likely to talk about what they themselves want? (Me, me, me!)

ⓘ Or about what they think or guess you or other people want?

ⓘ Or about what is (impersonally) required by eg the organization?

ⓘ And you?

ⓘ **So what conclusions can you draw about how exactly you have been communicating with each other and where you might have been at 'cross' purposes and what you might consider in the future?**

4. WHOSE 'ENEMY' IS IT ANYHOW?

It's inevitable that many people when feeling 'got at' will ask why does this always happen to *me*? And so it's important to find out whether this has been your own 'personal' enemy, or if they've been targeting others as well.

ⓘ Who else has been feeling 'got at' by this person? (NB If you don't feel it's appropriate for you to do this research yourself – eg by looking to see who else avoids the 'enemy', or who stops talking when they're around – then you could ask a 'friend' to help.)

5. WHO IS THIS 'ENEMY' SIMILAR TO?

Let's explore who this 'enemy' reminds you of, and how:

> 'When I go into past experiences I realize that they set the reaction to this *type* of person, eg whenever I meet a bombastic woman it reminds me of a fat aunt who terrified me. I then find out how other people deal with these difficult people – subtly though, not going about talking about them behind their back.'
>
> *'Francis'*

ⓘ Who exactly is this 'enemy' similar to or who do they remind you of? (There may be several people, ie a pattern here.)
ⓘ And in what ways, exactly?
ⓘ What is the learning from this?

6. AND WHERE ARE *YOU* COMING FROM?

This next section will enable you to play the part of a truly great investigative journalist, but please remind yourself of 'Top Tips for Information Gathering', page 127.

- ⓘ What is important to me about resolving this situation?
- ⓘ What have I been hoping for?
- ⓘ What have I been finding difficult?
- ⓘ What skills have I been missing or needing?
- ⓘ What information has been withheld from me or have I been missing or needing?
- ⓘ What else have I been missing or needing?
- ⓘ What has stopped me getting what I've needed or been missing?
- ⓘ What has been going against what I value or believe in or what's important to me?
- ⓘ What have I chosen not to admit to myself?
- ⓘ What exactly have I been scared of or worried about?
- ⓘ What have I been kidding myself about?!
- ⓘ Instead of asking myself *why* does/did this happen to me (victim-speak), *how* exactly (journalist-speak) did I find myself or get myself into this situation, do I think?
- ⓘ How exactly have I managed not to change the situation yet?
- ⓘ And what am I happy with and do *not* want to change?
- ⓘ So what do I suspect might be the six things I could do or say that *might* help the situation?
- ⓘ And what do I suspect might be the six things I could *stop* doing or saying that might help the situation?
- ⓘ And, finally, what *has* been going well, even though I might not have noticed at the time?
- ⓘ And, finally, finally, what observations might other people (eg wise and trusted friends or colleagues) make, from their own perspectives?

7. GETTING NEW PERSPECTIVES BY BEING IN OTHER PEOPLE'S SHOES

How many times have people ever said to us that we should

put ourselves in other people's shoes to see their side of the story?

'I see a number of different angles and viewpoints.'

'Harry'

'Try to understand them, why they're like they are and what could possibly influence them. Listen to them – if they'll share – and try to put oneself in their shoes; asking where they are trying to get to ultimately and how you can help them get there, if appropriate, without compromising yourself. Find common ground and don't let them get to you personally, keeping business objectives in mind.'

'Sheila'

'A good lesson is separating intent from behaviour – what's caused this person to be this way – is their intent to hurt me or is it something else? It's also about clarity of outcome – what do I want to achieve for me and them? Behind every behaviour is a positive intention, for that person, if not for me.'

'Charlie'

Putting ourselves in other people's shoes may seem easier said than done, but it's actually very easy to do.

1. Imagine seeing the other person (the 'enemy') and if this seems a bit daunting:
   ■ remember to keep a straight back, to keep the situation factual rather than emotional;
   ■ move them away to make them smaller – so that you can see them or hear them or just get a general feel for them at a distance that feels comfortable to you;
   ■ make them black and white and a still picture rather than big, bright and in your face;
   ■ turn down the sound, make them fuzzy or even put them behind a door for the time being. It's up to you. Whatever feels safe and comfortable.

2. Now ask yourself what, in this situation, are you:
   ① **thinking** – write down absolutely everything that comes to mind;

ⓘ **feeling** – it often takes a while for these to make themselves felt;

ⓘ **needing** – from them or indeed from anyone else.

3 Now imagine going over to where they were, and stand in their shoes, looking back at *you* in this situation. Again, you can adjust your size or other aspects of your appearance from where they are standing, as you ask yourself what you feel that *they* are:

ⓘ **thinking** – write down absolutely everything that comes to mind;

ⓘ **feeling** – again, it often takes a while for these bodily sensations to make themselves felt;

ⓘ **needing** – from you or indeed from anyone else.

4. Now imagine going to a new place in the position of a detached observer, from where you can see where both *you* are standing and where *they* are standing. Based on your observations when standing in your own and the other person's shoes – and remembering that this is just information at the moment, and you don't have to act on anything yet – just jot down how exactly the situation *might* be improved by what you might:

ⓘ **say;**

ⓘ **stop saying;**

ⓘ **do;**

ⓘ **stop doing;**

ⓘ **think** – ie say to yourself;

ⓘ **stop thinking** – ie stop saying to yourself;

ⓘ **believe to be true** – about yourself, the other players, the organization, life etc;

ⓘ **stop believing to be true** – about yourself, the other players, the organization, Life etc;

ⓘ **need;**

ⓘ **no longer need.**

5. By all means repeat the sequence, sleep on it, and talk the ideas through with other people. Then try these ideas on

for size, by going into a) your shoes and b) into the other person's shoes again to see what the ideas feel like. And make whatever adjustments you like. And keep writing down whatever else comes to mind.

'What has worked is looking at matters from the difficult person's point of view, and/or trying to understand why they are behaving in a 'difficult' way. For example, it has been useful for my management to think about the frustrations of a middle-aged man working at the same job for 20 years, with the prospect of another 20 years of the same. In that situation we need to find development opportunities and/or challenges that can potentially take the place of the difficult behaviour, and reinforce that person's confidence and self-esteem.'

'Rochelle'

8. KNOWING THE CURRENT CLIMATE WE'RE ALL WORKING IN

It's said that any fool can run an organization (including a team, a department, a country or even a family) when 'things' in general are going well. But when things are going badly or there are increased external pressures and everyone needs to pull together it can force people to work too closely together for comfort. When there was less pressure, some relationships were tolerable. With increased pressure, enmities can surface. It can be useful here, as anywhere, to state the obvious, eg 'While we're going through tough times, we obviously have to interact more. Maybe we can put aside any personal differences we have for the time being, and just focus on the task in hand, please?' So:

ⓘ **What evidence is there that times are tough – either overall or for individuals – and in what ways exactly has this affected a) me, b) the 'enemy' and c) 'things' in general?**

9. WHAT ARE MY HIDDEN BELIEFS THAT ARE HOLDING ME BACK?

It's really useful at this information-gathering stage to identify the hidden beliefs that are driving us (like a car's accelerator) and holding us back (like the brake) in 'enemy' situations like this. It's our positive beliefs that enable us to 'hold everything together' and our negative beliefs – in tough times – that make us feel wretched. But we can easily change them. (You don't believe me?! Read on.)

I've worked with many very skilled people who nevertheless believe about themselves eg 'I'm stupid' or 'I'm no good' or 'I'm not worth it.'

These beliefs generally come about like this:

1. someone in so-called authority – a teacher or parent or boss – said to us eg 'You're stupid';
2. we didn't realize that it was in a specific situation and what they really meant was eg 'You failed to understand that feature on the computer';
3. a few other incidents arose where we were again told that we were eg stupid and where again we failed to understand that it was in a specific context;
4. and then the big shift occurred as 'You are stupid' became internalized as 'I am stupid' and became a belief about our whole self, rather than opinions about eg computing skills;
5. and this 'belief' coloured many, many future situations.

Similarly, if someone tells us that we 'should' do X or Y, then, unless it's a sensible safety or health precaution, we need to hear it as advice, not internalize it as an 'I should'.

ⓘ So what are the Shoulds, Musts and other beliefs that I've been believing to be true regarding this 'enemy' situation?

ⓘ And, where appropriate, Who says? What would happen if I did (or didn't) do X? Who or what is stopping me doing what I feel is right?

10. IT'S FINE TO BE STUPID

Even though I don't like the word 'stupid', I'm very happy to admit to myself that I was stupid at not realizing X, or being able to do Y – and therefore I needed to get more informed or get more skilled at it – but it wasn't really stupidity, it was never having had the information or skills to handle the situation in the first place. Big deal!

So if we hear that we're eg stupid, we might ask ourselves or the other person eg 'at what, exactly, please?' and maybe add 'So please tell me what exactly to do to get it right (for you) next time?'

ⓘ Regarding this 'enemy' situation, what can I admit to factually, that I've not been able to admit to emotionally?

11. MY BEST BELIEFS ARE...

Now let's get some information on what you've been believing to be true, in your 'enemy' situation.

Here are some common beliefs, which might or might not apply to you, but they're just thought-starters: 'I'm not the sort of person who...' 'Changing your mind is a sign of weakness,' 'You should never back down,' 'Don't be stupid,' 'It's a sign of weakness to...' 'Grown men don't cry.'

ⓘ What have I been believing to be true, in general, about this situation?
ⓘ About the other person(s)?
ⓘ About my skills and abilities?
ⓘ About myself?

And now what are the beliefs you would *love* to have in 'enemy' situations (and yes, we *can* choose to believe whatever we want to believe – just look at politicians, so-called celebrities, and other self-deluded friends and family – I could go on!).

Again, here are some examples as thought starters: 'We're all on the same side,' 'This is about work, not about personality,' 'What they think of me is not who I am,' 'Everything passes,' 'I can just appear calm.' So:

ⓘ What do I *want* to believe, in general, about this situation from now on?
ⓘ About the other person(s)?
ⓘ About my skills and abilities?
ⓘ About myself?

12. ROLES

Whether we like it or not, we all play roles, both when we're with other people and even when we're on our own. We may not intend to, but it just happens. For example, we play different roles when we're eg with friends (playing the fool?), with children (acting responsibly?), or with bosses (respectful professional? rebellious child?). Or when we're feeling sorry for ourselves, we might be playing eg hurt child, or wounded but brave victim.

All of these help us to have a sense of who we are, or think we are, in the situation, and this naturally affects how we behave. Of course, we're just playing different parts in different situations, so we couldn't possibly sum up who we are as a person by just one of these roles, could we? Otherwise we'd be acting/feeling/thinking like eg a victim *all* of the time. Or playing the fool in every situation, regardless of how appropriate it might be.

And, yes, you've guessed it, some people *do* find that the role has taken them over. They 'can't help' playing the fool even in serious situations. Or they act like a victim even when out socially.

We can change the roles we play. We do this naturally with different people in different situations. It's called being flexible, or acting appropriately, as opposed to being inflexible and not 'fitting in' to the situation.

So:

ⓘ **What role(s) have I have been playing in this 'enemy' situation?** – and you can express these in any way you like, for example a *general* term such as 'victim' or something more specific such as 'Tom Cruise where he...' or 'Meryl Streep when she...'

13. AND FINALLY

ⓘ What have I overlooked? What is apparent to me now, that wasn't before?

ⓘ What was I assuming to be true, that might not have been true?

Part 4

Get Planning to Transform your 'Enemy' Situation Calmly

INTRODUCTION

Congratulations on your patience – many people want to leap into action before they're clear what needs acting upon and, therefore, in which direction they need to leap. (That's why we keep hearing eg 'Why can't I get this sorted out?' or 'Why does nothing work?')

Well, you've administered First Aid from Part 1 (The Ten Essential Survival Strategies).

You've chosen some Survive and Thrive Strategies from Part 2 (The Fifteen Toughest Types of 'Enemy').

And you've been Getting new information for new ways of moving forward from Part 3.

So *now* it's time to get planning.

28

Getting your Goal Plan Ready

Many people feel overwhelmed even at the thought of action *lists*, let alone actions, because they need a manageable first step, and to feel confident that it's going to work better than just putting up with things as they are. Also it's often much easier and more effective to *stop* doing something, rather than to do something new. And many ill-informed decisions get made when someone thinks they 'should' move quickly even though their own gut feel tells them otherwise. How many times do we hear after a disastrous decision, for example 'If only I'd known...' or 'Why didn't anyone warn me?' or 'I wish I'd followed my instinct'?

None of this is surprising because we're often told that we 'should' make decisions faster than we feel comfortable with, and also a typical action list or to-do list only covers one tenth of what's needed! What follows are, therefore, the full 10 categories that really need to be covered, and at this stage it's our 'could' list, rather than an 'action' list, as we need lots of options to choose from. And we're not going to have a daunting goal – if it was that simple you'd have achieved it already! We're going to develop a much more manageable 10-point goal plan.

And at this stage it's limited only to *what* you want, without worrying (yet) about *how* you might achieve it. Too many

plans never get started because we're thinking about *how* difficult it might be, without having clearly defined the 'it' in the first place!

First, though, it's important to know how to generate some options by systematic daydreaming!

'Minds are like parachutes, they only function when they are open.'

James Dewar

'If you only look at what is, you might never attain what could be.'

Anonymous

'Imagination is even more important than knowledge.'

Albert Einstein

Action Tip: **Daydream Out to your Right**

It's always fascinated me that many people say they get their best ideas lying on a beach or in bed or the bath (rarely, it seems, in meetings!) and for 95 per cent of the population, looking up and out to the *right* is their daydreaming planning-ahead space (just as 'putting things behind them' is behind their left shoulder, and 'feeling down' is associated with looking down). For the other 5 per cent the left and right spaces are reversed.

Things are looking up

I was having lunch with a friend and after a while, he said 'You are lucky, you know – I've never been able to see anything in the future for myself.' What fascinated me is that most people who talk about the future actually *look* at it – usually up and out to their right – but my friend was staring dejectedly down at the floor in the restaurant. Aha, I thought. I wonder if I can get him looking up, and if that's going to help. I poured some more wine, and said 'It's *really* frustrating, isn't it...' I banged the bottle back down on the table on the '*really*'. This might not have got him looking up, but at least it startled him away from his depressed fascination with the floor. I leaned back in my seat and kept talking, but looking and gesturing – rather exaggeratedly, I must admit – up at the ceiling to his right. And gradually, he leaned back as well and started looking up. And he started talking about what he'd like to do in the future, and carried on for a full 20 minutes. Until he suddenly said 'Gosh – what on earth has happened? I've never been able to do that!' 'It must be the wine,' I said.

So when we're deciding what we want, it's important that we have space to daydream, brainstorm and otherwise think about whatever works best for us. This might be a quiet spot in a garden, or whatever works best for you.

YOUR GOAL PLAN

'The very essence of leadership is that you have to have vision. You can't blow an uncertain trumpet.'

Theodore Hesburgh

'If you don't change direction you'll end up where you're going.'

Chinese proverb

So, in a quiet place, look up and out to the right and enjoy your daydreaming around the following. Then jot down *what* could improve the situation. Remember, you don't need to know at the moment *how* exactly you could achieve each of these, so write in whatever comes to mind, even so-called impossible thoughts. (And please note that the dreaded 'to do' is at the *end* of the ten areas!)

ⓘ What I could stop thinking (ie stop saying to myself).
ⓘ What I could think (ie say to myself).
ⓘ What role(s) I could stop playing.
ⓘ What role(s) I could play.
ⓘ What I could stop believing to be true.
ⓘ What I could choose to believe (about myself, other people, situations, life, fairness etc).
ⓘ What I could stop saying or writing.
ⓘ What I could say or write.
ⓘ What I could stop doing.
ⓘ What I could do.

And so, in a nutshell:

ⓘ What do I want for the team/department/organization?
ⓘ What do I want for me?

NB The above questions are based on the in-depth approach in *Coaching Made Easy* (Mike Leibling and Robin Prior, Kogan Page 2003).

Congratulations

You've just achieved something extraordinary – you've defined what you want, without using any jargon. You've defined a comprehensive *strategic goal plan* (ie what you want!) in terms of what role you need to play, and what you need to do, think, feel, and believe.

GETTING FAMILIAR WITH THE OUTCOME FROM YOUR GOAL PLAN

There's only one desirable outcome in any working situation and that is to establish:

■ a professional relationship;
■ with respectful behaviours; and
■ an absence of disrespectful behaviours.

This will ideally produce a *wonderful* working relationship, where everyone, especially you, will thrive professionally and personally.

Or maybe it's sufficient just to have a 'good enough' working relationship, where everyone will be OK, solely at the professional level.

Or maybe your best option, realistically, will be to have a distant relationship, where your best option is to go elsewhere emotionally, or even physically (ie leave), where you will be much happier.

What's absolutely certain is that an 'enemy' relationship cannot be desirable in the long term.

So, as with any journey, it's useful to know what the destination will be like, so we'll know when we've got there. And since the only ways we can sense anything are by what we see, hear, feel, smell and taste, when this 'enemy' situation is successfully sorted:

ⓘ What I'll be seeing is...
ⓘ What I'll be hearing is...
ⓘ What I'll be feeling is...
ⓘ What I'll be smelling is... – yes, some people can smell eg success, trouble
ⓘ What I'll be tasting is... – and yes, some people can taste eg victory.

Action Tip: Be Aware of Others' Outcomes Too

Sometimes, of course, there may be many things that we and the 'enemy' each want from a situation, and we'll need to negotiate.

For example, *you* might want to be left alone to concentrate on doing your job, while your boss might need frequent reassurance that it's going to plan. Or your boss might be happier with an inadequate job as long as an 'impossible' deadline is met, whereas *you* need to do a thorough job, even if it takes longer.

Without finding out what all the wants are, there's little chance of satisfying them all, of course. But – I hear you say – you have to compromise in the end anyway, don't you? No – I hear me reply – absolutely not: why settle for second best?

The question then becomes 'So how exactly can you, Boss, be satisfied that the work is going to plan, without interrupting my concentration frequently? What could we agree to?' or 'How exactly can I give you the good work you need by your deadline, and perhaps give you the rest later?'

Action Tip: Invite Other People's Ideas

When I hear people say 'Why on earth didn't I think of that myself?!' I usually find it was because they were too close to the situation in question – in fact they were *in* it: they literally 'couldn't see the wood for the trees'. And however hard we try to see all sides of a situation, we can often see only what's immediately in front of us, especially if we've been feeling trapped and unable to move around to see all sides of the story.

And so I find it invaluable to explain to a few people what I'm struggling with, and to ask for as many ideas as possible before deciding upon a course of action.

I'll take on board their ideas as 'maybes' – rather than 'shoulds' – until I have at least three that feel good to me. I'll thank them for their ideas, and change the subject. This is not a discussion group, so I don't need to explain what I think of each suggestion or what I'm going to do with it – indeed, I probably don't know yet. I simply say 'thank you' to each one, and wait for the next one.

How to (not) deal with this bully

I once had a customer who I found very difficult and I didn't want to deal with him. He was the biggest bully I've ever met, and to give you an idea, he deliberately stressed out one of his staff to such a degree that the poor man was hospitalized and he then tried to get his wife to have an affair with him. Anyway. He was a big customer, and I was given no choice but to get on with him.

So I got a group of colleagues together, and briefed them that I wanted some ideas, please, on *how* I can deal with this person, comfortably. I didn't go into lots of detail, but asked for lots of 'Maybe you could...' or 'How would it be if...' ideas, and smiled sweetly and said 'Thank you' to each one (and translated internally any 'should', 'must', 'why on earth didn't you' etc suggestions into little Maybes and Perhaps in my mind!).

Several (uncensored) ideas felt appealing, including:

■ perhaps you could just grin and bear it? (but not any more, I couldn't);

■ maybe you could take out a contract on him? (quite appealing but unethical);

■ maybe you shouldn't work with him at all? (very appealing, but I wanted to keep my job);

and then

■ you get on well with his PA so maybe you could just communicate through her?

And so, from that moment on, I would ring her each morning and she would consult with him, and she would ring me back with requests and instructions. She was a charming conduit, and on the rare occasions that I met with her boss I found that her charm had somehow softened my animosity towards him. Result.

Action Tip: **Get a Supporter or Two**

The only thing worse than feeling 'got at' is feeling got at and alone.

Since no one is 100 per cent skilled at handling absolutely everything, there's no loss of face in discussing possibilities with each other, so we should make sure we have supporters or friends with whom we can talk through our plans. It's good to have to think aloud. Or we can compose our thoughts in an e-mail and send it (only) to ourselves. How can we know what we think unless we hear or see what we have to say?!

Action Tip: **Make Sure you're Getting What you Want**

Quite simply, it's essential to fix a time (each afternoon? each Friday afternoon? both?) to check that you're getting what you want in progressing this 'enemy' situation and then making any adjustments necessary.

(I hear you asking 'Why not review progress conventionally – in the *mornings*, or *Monday* mornings?' Well, what's the point in planning our day or week when it's already started?! Like this we can get it sorted in time to have a nice evening and a good night's sleep and an enjoyable weekend, by getting it off our mind, and knowing what we'll be doing next.)

29

Making your Goal Plan Happen and Getting What you Want

Remember that the best time to deal with a difficult situation has passed. The second best time is now. So review your wants, make any additions and changes that feel right to you, and highlight the really appealing ones.

Then jot down *how* exactly you might go about achieving what appeals to you. And for those where you're asking yourself 'But how on earth could I ever...?!' – take yourself literally, and answer it!

Rupert's question

I was meeting some friends for lunch. Rupert arrived first and was asking about my new role at work. I told him I was really enjoying it, travelling the world, and working with really interesting people and situations. 'What could be better?' he asked me. 'Exactly,' I replied. 'Er, no, Mike,' he continued, and then looked me in the eye and asked *'What* could be better?' I had to stop and think. 'Er, more nights in my own bed, I suppose.' He paused, then still looking me in the eye asked 'So what are

> you going to *do* about it, Mike?' And I heard my voice, quietly and calmly say 'I'm going to resign, Rupert.' And as I said it, the light seemed brighter, and something hopped over my left shoulder – a decision, it was later explained to me!

So, if you're asking yourself 'How on earth could I ever...?' daydream out to your right, and answer your question with some coulds or mights. Jot them down later if you like and then play with these ideas for at least one overnight, to see how they sound and feel in the morning.

> 'The mind, once expanded to the dimensions of larger ideas, never returns to its original size.'
>
> *Oliver Wendell Holmes*

KEEP PLAYING WITH YOUR GOAL

Be absolutely clear on what you want and keep reminding yourself.

Do not under any circumstances let practicalities water down what you want. What you want is what you want, or need, or must have. There will be plenty of time to deal practically with *how* you achieve what you want, in due course.

The archer

I knew someone who was an archer. When asked how good he was he would modestly say that if there was a target he was number four in the UK. But he would then add, with a smile on his face, 'But if there's no target, who knows?'

Live with it. Play with it. Change it to feel even more comfortable with it. Sleep on it. Tell it to other people so that you can hear yourself say it aloud, and they can ask you useful questions about it. All of this will help to make it more solid and more real (ie more thought through).

■ Be clear (really clear).
■ Be cooperative (properly so).
■ Be nice.
■ Be forgiving (never hold a grudge for even a second).
■ Be yourself.

'Edward'

Action Tip: **Sleep on it**

Several people I know will say to themselves, when about to go to sleep for the night, that they'd like to wake up in the morning, please, with some ideas about how exactly they could go about X. And, sure enough, the subconscious works on it as they sleep (and often they say that they sleep better because it's not 'on their mind' all night).

Action Tip: **Take a Bit More Time to Think, for a Change**

'The dance becomes thicker and gluier the longer it goes on – so I don't have to make an instant decision – I can take time out to decide what's going on and how to deal with it, eg is it about helping *me* change (behaviours/attitudes) or them?'

'Virginia'

CONSIDER SOMETHING DIFFERENT THIS TIME

Do something different – this often throws other people

completely. It may not only take the wind out of their sails, but take their sails out of the wind altogether!

You know the old saying, 'If at first you don't succeed, try, try and try again.' Well, this is one of the most dangerous sayings I know:

■ it suggests that we should succeed first time, whereas many situations need eg time to consult, time to think, perseverance, learning, a drip-drip approach;

■ 'try, try and try again' suggests that it's going to be hard work, whereas most truly effective solutions are simple and elegant, not trying;

■ if at first I didn't succeed, what's the point of trying it again? I should try something *different*; and finally

■ I've found time and time again that what works for me is generally *stopping* doing/saying/thinking/trying, rather than trying yet another something new.

Action Tip: Ask the Opposite

I always used to ask visiting vegetarians/vegans 'What don't you eat?' and got a long list of what I should avoid cooking, but not much idea of what I could cook for them. I now ask them to tell me what they *do* like to eat. Much easier all round. Maybe try to ask or do the opposite of what you've been doing up to now?

Action Tip: If in Doubt, Say or Do Nothing

'I had an angry customer with friends backing her up. I took the full force of verbal abuse over a full 30 minutes. With hindsight I realized after the first five minutes of foul language, threatening behaviour, spitting, there was nothing left to say or do except kill me! The other 25 minutes were mere repetition. Remember, this is about a dress. I took this personally, and I never should have let that happen.

I was shaken and very upset. However, looking at it a different way I didn't say anything back because I couldn't promise anything on behalf of the company. If I had confronted her instead with the cold hard facts and said all that was going through my mind, one of us would have been hurt; over a dress. If I think about that it makes me smile and I'm glad I couldn't respond in the moment. I came out the winner here and she got her dress but looks stupid in it.'

'Susannah'

Action Tip: If the Situation was Oral, Put It in Writing

'Well, it's hard to change a system or an individual's take on it overnight, so most of the time I find myself shutting up and taking it on the chin. However, I am often tempted to clarify in writing (if words fail me at the time) how the situation looks from my side. While the note might never be read or understood by the person in question, it would help to sort through the sequence of events in my own mind and bring closure by "being heard".'

'George'

Action Tip: If the Situation was Public, Do It in Private

'When I have been drawn into an argument out of frustration, usually because the other person won't let go of a point when I want to move on, it's almost like they are used to winning arguments and won't give up until they get their own way, which just winds me up further, and moves me from being consultative to being directive. I now say less, let them exhaust themselves, and/or adjourn the meeting, and speak to the person outside the meeting, checking in with how they are feeling. There is often an underlying issue!'

'Melissa'

Action Tip: **If the Situation was Private, Do It in Public**

If the enemy's approach is to do their dirty work in private, or to spread rumours or gossip in private, one-to-one, then they are hoping that people won't compare notes and rumble their little game.

And so it might work very well to bring it out in the open, to close down their game. It's useful to let them know that you're aware of this, in a public arena (no, not necessarily Wembley Stadium or Madison Square Gardens – a corridor will do) with other people around so that they know that people are aware of their actions, and that you're being completely in the open with everyone. This can be done nicely, of course, eg 'Thanks very much for letting me know that I'm in trouble with "Jim" but I'm a big boy now and can sort matters out for myself, thank you.' And I will generally square the circle by later seeing the rumour-monger in private on a one-to-one basis, and looking them in the eye will say that I know they meant well (even if I believe that they meant well only for their own selfish reasons) but I'm not going to need this sort of help any more, thank you. OK? – and the rhetorical question at the end is the clincher.

But what do I say when I *next* meet them, I hear you ask! Well, personally, I want to think I've drawn the line under this situation and have moved on, and so I'd say something like 'Pat,' – because calling someone by name and pausing a little, while looking them in the eye is making *real* I-contact – 'I've drawn a line under the situation and want to move on in a good professional way now, OK?' and then I'd change the subject to prove the point, even if it's just a 'see you later' or similar. And, by the way, tagging an 'OK' or similar onto a statement or question can be really powerful, can't it? It gets someone questioning for themselves what you've just said, doesn't it? And while they're doing that, you can just pop in your change of subject to settle the matter in their mind once and for all. Can't you?! Right. Onto the next tip!

Action Tip: **If the Situation is very Emotional, 'Go Formal'**

Sometimes 'going formal' with a facilitator is the best way to get results, when two people can't see the same wood for the same trees. And asking for some form of dispute resolution such as mediation or arbitration can be a really useful way of saying to an organization 'This is not my problem (even though it had obviously felt like it!) or at least it's not down to me to fix a situation between two employees, so can *you* get it sorted, please?'

'I managed these through a formal process, with HR involved, setting clear behavioural goals and more clarity around their role and responsibilities, putting them in the positive. I provide, model and keep to clear consistent boundaries, for myself too. This is essential, to ensure a more consistent level of performance and behaviour so that people know where they are with you and can better know what to expect. I also ensure they are getting the support they need from both me and the team around them, through more regular formal catch-ups but also more informal support from within the team.'

'Sheila'

'The HR department, the secretary and I had a review, and hammered out a compromise. She was a reasonable secretary when she stuck to secretarial matters for the staff she liked, so she did the work for half the department; and the other half, including me, who found her difficult, had a different secretary.'

'Francis'

'Attitudes get set, both the "difficult" person's and those expected to deal with that person. If there is to be any progress, the mould must be broken. Specifically, we like to be clear about what outcome we are trying to achieve from our dealings with the "difficult" person. Then handle our behaviour to try and get that result. If, as we have done several times, it can be agreed by all that we dump the history, and start with a clean slate, that can be very successful in moving forward constructively.'

'Edward'

'I had incredible back-up from my line manager so I never had a "face-to-face" meeting with them about all their issues. It was taken out of my hands completely.'

'Rochelle'

Action Tip: **The Politics of Envy – Make them Jealous**

'I gave lots of attention to someone else instead, working closely and successfully with another director. Then the "problem" one got jealous and was all open arms!'

'Tamatha'

Action Tip: **Give them the Benefit of the Doubt**

'I think it's worth remembering that difficult people are often stressed and cannot cope. What difficult people need most is help. They just don't know why, or feel stupid or don't even know how to ask for help. Difficult people are ignorant people desperate for someone to be with them in that moment. They are also the hardest to help and the hardest to love and be kind to, which is what they need. Every day I understand how stupid I am not to have been looking after myself but numerous difficult people instead.'

'George'

GETTING YOUR ACTIONS IN ORDER

Here's a deceptively simple template for deciding what to do and in what order.

ⓘ Start by defining what you want to achieve and what the situation will be like when you've achieved it.
ⓘ Now define how it is, at the moment.
ⓘ And now define what the situation will be like when you're *halfway* there.

ⓘ And what will it be like when you're halfway between halfway and your goal?

ⓘ And what will it be like when you're halfway between now, and halfway?

The more you can consider each of these, the better. And – for each one – you can add in what you'll need, and make getting that help or support an integral part of your journey:

> 'How many times do we hear the cry that there's never enough time for training and development and team building? And yet I would guarantee anyone in any organization that an hour well invested will save so much time and heartache and frustration.'
>
> *'Brian'*

> 'One answer might have been to attend assertiveness training earlier in my working career.'
>
> *'Larry'*

(And, shh, don't tell anyone who's nervous about Next Steps, that's exactly what the last ⓘ is, isn't it?!)

30

Thinking the Unthinkable

So you thought that this book was all about how to survive and thrive when working with the enemy?! Well, just to be realistic, none of us can change the world and it's only realistic to consider that life might be considerably better if we change *our* world instead.

Action Tip: **We Don't Need to be Perfect**

Always remember 'I am enough':

'It has been helpful to understand and accept that we can't always be right, and indeed don't always have to be right.'

'Edward'

Action Tip: **Whistleblowing**

If someone tells tales on someone else, or blows the whistle on unethical practices, they are known as a 'whistleblower' (or worse) and often shunned as a traitor in public, whilst admired by fellow-sufferers in private. It's similar if someone takes their organization to court. And because the language is very personal, at identity level (eg 'a whistleblower') that's why people, and organizations, take it very personally.

So, just as an organization needs a policy on bullying, we need a public and published policy on whistleblowing.

But I really dislike the term 'whistleblower', as it's wholly inappropriate to most situations, since it suggests that there's something disruptive and loud, disturbing the peace. But the reality of the situation is far removed from this description. There is unease, not peace, and the 'whistleblower' has chosen to reveal (usually quietly, at least at first) the truth that many others have known or suspected, but no one has addressed. It's like the story of the young child who says what everyone else was thinking: that the emperor who bought beautiful new clothes from a trickster actually bought nothing and was exposed. Similarly, it's the *situation* that exposes the organization, not the 'whistleblower'.

And that's how it's best addressed – revealing what's already there, as an impersonal 'big picture' concern rather than as a personal attack, eg 'I know we all believe in fair trading/treatment/behaviour and that none of us would want the organization to be seen in any other light. Maybe it would be prudent, therefore, for us to have a regular audit of practices, with independent contributors (from outside, or from other parts of the organization) to ensure that we can be proud of all of our practices? If anyone has any counter-proposals please let me/us know so that we can draw up a policy and procedures for these audits.'

In many organizations this is done as part of their Best Practice Auditing. And maybe 'Best Practice Auditing' should replace the term 'whistleblowing'?!

Action Tip: Think Carefully about Involving HR

HR (which used to be called Personnel) is generally charged with protecting the organization's interests, rather than individuals' interests, although both are important, of course. You may have an HRD person (Human Resources Development – which used to be called Training) who can help in confidence. Or an EAL or EAP (Employee Assistance Line or Programme) who you can speak to in confidence. Or a staff representative, who you can also speak to in confidence, and who might be able to accompany you to meetings as your supporter. Or a trade union representative.

It's worth finding out what's available to you, for information only at this stage. And it's a good time to get information on your organization's published policies on eg grievance-handling and bullying so that you know how they are handled where you are. Most decent-sized organizations have them, and you can always enquire about them very nonchalantly, yes? If your organization does not have any published policies, then you can always find some on the internet to see what's possible. In this way *if* you choose to make any formal complaint, then you can ensure that there's a procedure for everyone to follow, to take the emotion out of it as much as possible. Or – if there is no procedure – you can offer what you've found, so that everyone knows the process.

But, having high hopes of HR can lead to disappointment, sometimes even bitter disappointment, since – after all – it's always pronounced Human *Resources*, not *Human* Resources, isn't it?

'It would have been good to understand much earlier in my career how damaging HR is to any professional. HR is probably the biggest source of dissatisfaction within a company.'

'Francis'

Action Tip: Getting out may Truly be your Best Option

I once saw a great production of *The Comedy of Errors* (which could sum up many episodes in my life, but this was the Shakespeare play). The two masters were chasing the two slaves around and around the stage, until they cornered them right at the front of the stage with nowhere to go. Until, that is, the cheeky slaves jumped up in the air and landed not on the stage but down with the audience, much to the bemusement of the two masters. And the audience. We can do that too. If things get too much for us, we can get out. We should always remember this. Of course there will be many considerations, but these could be easier to solve than the stress, strokes, heart attacks etc that might happen if we choose to stay on this particular stage. At least we can choose to get out, with our dignity intact, and be able to say 'Thank goodness I got out before it was too late' rather than wait for the indignities of who-knows-what to happen to us.

After all, it's only worth spending so much time and energy on a situation, and there are some situations where the best option might be to walk away. For example, if an organization behaves in a way that's uncomfortable for us, given our values, why on earth are we staying there?

In situations like these I think of the expression that there are three reasons never to try to teach a pig to fly:

- we won't succeed;
- it'll be really hard work;
- we'll really annoy the pig!

Let's be honest (and realistic) – this job might have been fine when we chose it, but every day when we wake up and go to work, it's like we're choosing it all over again. But why on earth should it still fit our needs?! We've moved on, the organization has moved on, and maybe it's time for us to move out, into a place that better fits our *current* needs?

Getting out is actually not the last resort for many people. The last resort for many people is to keep suffering – with all the consequent health and relationship implications. (Although with 'getting out' there will of course be other considerations, but nothing that cannot be overcome.)

'I realized after nine months (it should have been after nine days, if not nine minutes!) that – realistically – I couldn't change the whole organization. It was bigger than I was. My boss was the problem. His boss wouldn't see me without my boss present. So that made him part of the problem too. I decided to stop there and get out.'

'Keith'

'I think I had had enough of delegation without recognition. I was probably ready to move on.'

'Tamatha'

'One job, the only answer was to resign. There was no way the person in charge of the project was ever going to allow me, a woman, any role or job.'

'Sheila'

'I might have to learn the lesson that walking away is also an option!'

'Charlie'

'You can test drive a car but you can't test drive a job. If you've bought a lemon get rid of it before there's even more to regret.'

'Francis'

'It's no defeat to advance to the next stage in your career.'

'George'

'It's not admitting defeat, it's just not for me any more.'

'Keith'

'If the going was rough, it was better to leave earlier than to have the upset of doing the fight, and finding nothing could be changed.'

'Edward'

'Walking away from the relationship and recognizing that's it's OK for me to say I've had enough doesn't mean I've "failed".'

'Patricia'

'I need to develop better judgement on when to stand back or walk away.'

'Larry'

Action Tip: And Now Review Again the Part 1 and Part 2 Strategies and Tips...

...to see which can be useful to you as you are moving forward. Go well!

Index

ALSO AVAILABLE FROM KOGAN PAGE

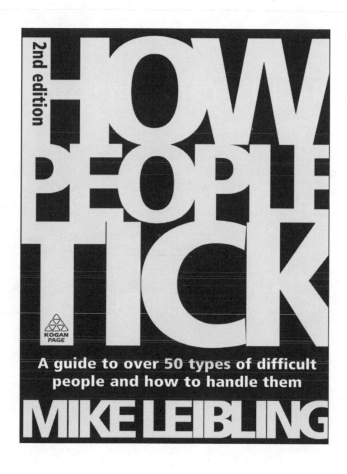

ISBN: 978 0 7494 5459 3   Paperback   2009

www.koganpage.com

One website.

A thousand solutions.